Reflections on Youth and Maturity

James K. Weber, M.D.

ARCHWAY
PUBLISHING

Archway Publishing books may be ordered through booksellers or by contacting:

Archway Publishing
1663 Liberty Drive
Bloomington, IN 47403
www.archwaypublishing.com
844-669-3957

Illustrations by Oatley Kidder

Scripture taken from the King James Version of the Bible.

ISBN: 978-1-6657-0854-8 (sc)
ISBN: 978-1-6657-0853-1 (hc)
ISBN: 978-1-6657-0855-5 (e)

Library of Congress Control Number: 2021912694

Print information available on the last page.

Archway Publishing rev. date: 07/30/2021

Dedicated to ZsaZsa and minette
—former Muses, now Angels—
and Louis, who lovingly succeeds them.

All of my best writing has been done
with these treasures at my side.

CONTENTS

Foreword

He gave up general surgery to teach yoga. That's the tagline, but Jim Weber's life story is only getting started. Add singer, swim meet official, classical music lover, houseboat husband, four-daughter father—Jim Weber has packed a lot into one life, and many of the choicest moments he has ladled into this quirkily charming memoir: *Joie de Vivre, As I See It.*

As if he's not interesting enough himself, Weber introduces us to a cast of characters and moments that keep the pages turning: the fellow who believed Satan inhabited his cell phone…The Man Who Can't Make Up His Mind (caps mine)…a game called "Poopy Foopy" (don't ask)… The Greatest Behind-the-Back Peanut Bag Tosser of All Time…not to mention musings on Beethoven, angels, and rainbows. Awareness and appreciation, really.

But perhaps the author's grandest achievement is his marriage to celebrated etiquette maven, Mary Mitchell. And what a relief to learn that someone so professionally proper on one occasion attempted to mount a bicycle, only to suffer the ignominy of her tush flying over the bike seat and landing on the ground. Typical of what's to be found in these pages: imperfect humanity.

Besides each other, the love of Mary and Jim Weber's life is their dog, Louis le Premier du Lac. It is during walks with Louis that Weber, ever paying attention, collects some of his most page-worthy moments.

The reading comes in fabulous fragments. It hopscotches all over time and place. Just go along for the ride and have fun. The author will connect the dots for you.

Jerry Spinelli is a Newbery Award-winning author of 35 books for young adults, including *Maniac Magee*, *Stargirl* (now a Disney movie), and *Crash* (also produced as a play). His autobiography, *Knots in My Yo-yo String* tells you pretty much all you need to know. He is married to Eileen Spinelli, herself a celebrated writer of children's books and an honoree at the White House reception for former First Lady Laura Bush's literary initiative.

Prologue

Jim Weber—more properly known as "Dr. James Weber"—has done the near-impossible: from a potpourri of sketches and musings he has fashioned a memoir that would entertain readers far beyond the purviews of family and close friends. This physician, surgeon, yoga instructor, father, traveler, and writer has produced a frank and highly readable saga that touches on (and occasionally punches) a wide variety of subjects, all drawn from real life.

We hear about Dreadful Cars He Has Known, early misbehavior at summer camp, catching a foul ball from Omar Vizquel, officiating as a swim meet judge, driving on the wrong side of the road when abroad, and motoring in historic downtown Florence. We also hear about life as a yoga instructor, reconnecting with the love of his life, remodeling a Seattle houseboat, traveling with a nonagenarian friend, meeting neighborhood characters, passport difficulties, and a close encounter with a bison—not to mention singing in the Yale Glee Club for a Beethoven's Ninth at Carnegie Hall under the legendary maestro Leopold Stokowski.

Witty and frank, this eminent former surgeon is not above the occasional pun. My favorite, on the subject of piano lessons: "Although I was not cut out to be a pianist, I did go on to cut out quite a few organs." Here's hoping you will find the puns, and the entire narrative, as entertaining as I have.

Melinda Bargreen's unfailingly constructive, prize-winning music critiques for *The Seattle Times* have delighted and informed readers for many years. In addition to writing *50 Years of Seattle Opera* and *Classical Seattle*, which profiles major figures in Seattle's music world, she has been awarded for her choral compositions. She has a doctorate in English literature from the University of California, Irvine.

Introduction

One of my first yoga therapy clients—an exemplary enthusiast of life—while dying from advanced prostate cancer, gave me a little book by Willard Spiegelman called *Seven Pleasures: Essays on Ordinary Happiness.*

Spiegelman advocates for seven pastimes, which he labels "pleasures." They are reading, walking, looking, dancing, listening, swimming, and writing. He devotes a chapter to each. I embrace his list, even while acknowledging that swimming is difficult in these pandemic times.

In browsing through the following pages, you will find varying degrees of emphasis on each of these pastimes, to which I add three more of particular import to me: teaching, collecting, and reflecting. The last of these is the *sine qua non* for what this book is all about.

Any exuberance you might detect in these compositions can be explained by the fact that all were written during a burst of creativity, the likes of which I never have experienced. The vignettes, anecdotes, stories, and essays almost wrote themselves, as I sat there taking a kind of mental—at times, emotional—dictation. Essentially,

I functioned like a scribe recording a series of events I had witnessed.

The entirety of this book came into being in the space of less than four months, in the midst of the worldwide coronavirus scourge. I was grateful for any productive work to perform while social distancing. Teaching yoga classes by Zoom was salutary, and writing was exhilarating. Frankly, I hardly could keep up with this sustained wave of inspiration.

These stories and essays are not intended to instruct. They were written purely for the joy of writing and the desire to entertain. If nothing else, they will give you some idea of how my mind works.

Although I factor in all the tales, I am not always the main character. My parents appear, along with my brother, my wife, daughters, assorted friends—human and otherwise—and acquaintances. New York City and baseball often play a part. Musical, historical, and literary heroes add their flavor to the stew.

Welcome to my life!

I. Here and There

My First (and Worst) Car Ever

When I tell anybody about the first car I ever had, I almost always forget about the first car before that other first car. Not surprisingly, I have owned more than a few autos in my life.

For thirty-five years or so, it seemed like all I ever drove was a Volvo. A green 142 sedan was the progenitor of the pattern. My parents bought it for me my junior year at Yale.

I think my mother was afraid that I would ask to borrow her Jaguar again to drive my singing group down to, around in, and back from Florida over Spring Break. I never told her about zooming across the state on Interstate 10 at one hundred miles per hour (or getting passed by a pickup truck going even faster). My mother is long gone now, so I can write about that. I suppose I also should admit to mooning a few toll booths we passed through, several times without paying.

Having gotten those puerile transgressions off my chest, I feel ready to go further back—another three years. I was hired as a camp counselor at my old summer camp in Maine. I had spent five previous summers there, four as a camper, and the previous year as a junior counselor.

By the way, junior counseling is not all it is cracked up to be. You end up with pretty much the same responsibilities as the counselors, while netting $36.24 for the eight weeks. I hope the pay scale has kept up with cost of living, and that JC's can reasonably expect a hundred or two today. But not at Great Oaks Camp. The place was sold twenty years ago and is now an apartment complex abutting Saturday Lake, every day, if the lake hasn't been converted to condominiums.

I had been a model camper. I even won the coveted Oak Leaf Cluster award when I was fifteen, by accumulating enough points in the only six activities I was good in to pass the minimum threshold. This was my crowning achievement. Sometimes I think it has been pretty much downhill for me ever since.

As a junior counselor, I was led astray by one Phil Ruggiero. A man who was accurately described by his first wife as "crude, loud and boisterous," who found for his second wife, after much looking, a woman who has to be more than a little hard of hearing. This man came, or I should say, burst into my life.

Phil hailed from Bogota, New Jersey and therefore was, by any New Yorker's definition, and in fact, a terrible driver. For some unknown reason, his father entrusted him with the old family Mercury that first summer we bonded.

Phil managed to force a piston through the cam

shaft—or something like that—of the much-loved, and now much-abused, Mercury. He asked me, "Do you hear that awful sound?"

Ever helpful, albeit ignorant about automobile mechanics, I suggested, "Just roll up the windows so you don't have to listen."

Moments later, the car died.

We were on our way back to camp after a night of drunken debauchery, outside Gray, which is not godforsaken, because there is at least one church there. I know this because we took turns sleeping on the concrete steps outside the church doors, while the other remained vigilant in an attempt to hitch a ride back to camp.

There were only a few thousand people living, if you can call it that, in Gray, and it's a safe bet that none of them were up at 2 a.m., when they "roll up the sidewalks," as my father used to say, dismissively, about small-town America, where vibrant night life is not to be found. We did manage to cadge a ride about five hours later from the only truck to rumble by all night.

We pulled into camp just in time for breakfast, while the Mercury was towed to a junkyard.

I was more than a little surprised that the camp director invited us back, considering the number of eyebrow-raising capers we cut that year, which I will not bore you with. Well, except for this one.

We invented a game called Poopy Foopy. The game, only for counselors (Read: Phil and me), took place in the bathroom, in adjoining stalls. The idea was to toss a foop (for those of you not in the know, the cardboard core of a toilet paper roll) over the partition.

The "recipient" (you haven't lived until you have had one tossed at you) would have to sit on the toilet seat without flinching. The foop would either strike some part of you, or it would miss. Hitting your opponent scores a point. And so forth. To and fro, the foop would go.

Which is all the kids could see, as they obediently stood outside the stalls and watched. As boring as this may seem, they all clearly preferred this activity to straightening up their bunks for inspection.

Wouldn't you know it? When the camp director showed up for a rare surprise inspection, none of the campers were in their cabins, because they were all in the bathroom, watching the foop fly and lustily cheering for their favorite contestant—obviously me, or I wouldn't be telling you all this.

Yes, to answer the question you should be asking yourself at this moment, we had a commissioner to arbitrate disputes, which were frequent and often heated. Issues like, "You flinched," or, "You peeked to see where I was sitting" (as if there were any other place to sit).

At any rate, the camp director was somewhat put out, even though Phil offered him a front row seat. He had seen enough and peremptorily banned the competition. The kids were ordered back to their cabins.

Dress inspection happened daily for the remaining

five weeks of camp, during which time Phil and I more or less minded our p's and q's. However, I think the reasons that we were invited back the next year were (a) the camp director and Phil were nextdoor neighbors, and (b) in his mind, we were pretty much of a package deal.

A year later, I was a full counselor and desperately in need of transportation to Maine. I had a bona fide NY Driver's License and forty-five dollars in my wallet, borrowed from my parents to cover my expenses until my first paycheck.

Mind you, passing the driving test in New York City is no easy feat. The testing officials, at least in my day, were tough. And sneaky. For instance, they would direct you to the only stop sign in Manhattan—almost always disguised by double-parked trucks, so that you could hardly ever see it—and sneer as you had to slam on the brakes at the last minute to avoid going right past it. Then they would have you attempt to parallel park in the tightest possible spot.

More than likely, you would not pass. Maybe, not on the second try either. My father, however, was determined that his boy would pass on the first go. He enrolled me in a driving school, after already having taught me pretty much everything I needed to know.

The driving school offered a refund if you failed the test, which they weren't about to let happen. I think several of the instructors were moonlighting NYC test officials. They alerted their students to all the tricks and pitfalls.

Anyway, I passed.

You know, NYC drivers are actually pretty good. They have to be, what with all the taxicabs, jitneys, and Ubers darting across lanes to pick up fares; all the jaywalkers; and all the construction going on. Add to that the ambulances trying to pick their way through the wall-to-wall traffic and everybody riding their horns, and you get the picture.

New Yorkers know full well that they are better drivers than the clowns from New Jersey or Massachusetts. Just ask them.

Phil and I were at a used car lot operating out of a gas station in Hackensack. The salesman showed us a few decent-looking cars, all of which were way beyond our budget. Once he knew that, he took us back behind the building, where he had one other car, a forlorn '56 Chevy Bel Air two-toned wagon. We "kicked the tires," looked under the hood like we know what we were doing, drove it around the block, and bought the car with our pooled finances—for all of fifty dollars.

The man quickly pocketed the cash, as if he were afraid that we might change our minds, and, just as we were about to pull out of the lot, asked, "So where are you all going with this car?"

"Maine."

His eyes widened. He said, "Well…good luck!"

With that benediction of sorts, we laughed nonchalantly and headed north.

Just barely onto the Connecticut Turnpike, Phil calmly said to me, "Jim, don't look now, but I think the gas pedal just fell off."

"Let me take a look." I scrambled down on the floor. No bucket seats in a '56 Chevy.

"Yeah. It's off."

"Do you think I ought to pull over?"

"Nah. Maybe I can put it back on. Keep going." And I did. And we did.

And it stayed on, most of the time. As long as you remembered to depress it while angling your foot to the left side. Any pressure applied from the right, and off it would fall.

We stopped at the next service station, since the used car dealership left only a small amount of gas in the car.

"You want I should check under the hood?" We told the attendant to go ahead.

"Radiator needs water. Brake fluid is low. So is the transmission fluid."

All fluids refilled in due course; off we went. At the next fill up, recalling the last words from the used car guy, I suggested we check under the hood again.

"Transmission fluid level is low."

"How low? We just had it topped up."

"Really low. You know you are leaking fluid under this car?"

"Is it transmission fluid?"

"Yup."

"Anything else?"

"Yup. Radiator's leaking water."

"Are we leaking gas, too?"

"Nope. Don't think so. Where are you headed?"

"Maine."

No comment. Just the wide eyes again.

Believe it or not, we made it to Maine. So what if we had to put transmission fluid in every time we gassed up? We only had to put water in the radiator every other time.

We felt that we would have full return on our investment if we could drive the car up to Maine, maintain it through the summer, and get it back home again. Then we would have to figure out what to do with it.

A day or two into the camp season we brought the car to a transmission repair shop and made inquiries.

"You are kidding, right?"

"What do you mean?"

"This car isn't worth it. Just keep replacing the transmission fluid."

The problem, as if there weren't enough problems already, was that other counselors were always after us to borrow the car for a night on whatever town they could manage to find near East Otisfield. We would tell them how to keep the gas pedal from falling off and get them to promise to fill all fluids before (hopefully) returning the car.

I actually drove it by myself one evening, on a date

with some girl I had met at the Italian hero sandwich shop in South Paris. She said the car had a funny smell. Like old socks. I hadn't noticed. The other issues occupied my attention.

Now that she mentioned it, I looked under the front and back seats, but couldn't find much more than a few pieces of popcorn, two Drive-In movie theater ticket stubs, and three M&Ms (two plain, one peanut). No socks. That was about the extent of our date, too, except that she made me treat her to a hero sandwich before she would tell me her name.

The hero tasted so good to her that she volunteered her phone number, not that I had asked.

She mentioned, between munches, that she was in a marching band. I told Phil. He told me that I had to cultivate the relationship. I tended to disagree, until he explained his reasoning.

"Maybe you can get her to bring the band to Great Oaks Camp some time. You know, on a practice run." Phil had played in a marching band in Bogota, and therefore was a kindred spirit to this girl. He might have been otherwise inclined, had he seen her. Frankly, was she not much to look at. Slim pickings in South Paris.

Presto! One day, a marching band showed up at the gate of Great Oaks Camp. We hadn't told anyone they were coming.

The camp director rolled his eyes, immediately surmising who had to have been behind this, and let them march in. The kids loved it; this was way better than watching us play Poopy Foopy. Phil and I became legends in our own time.

Camp season ended, and, two-thirds done with our investment, we were on our way home. I wouldn't say that we were exactly optimistic about our chances, yet the old car had demonstrated a surprising degree of pluck. We very nearly made it, too.

Remember the tires that we kicked in Bogota, NJ? Perhaps we should have looked closer at the nearly non-existent treads. We had a blowout just before getting on the highway in Maine. Fortunately, we had made sure that the car came complete with a spare tire. Finding the air pressure to be more than a bit low, we pulled into the next service station to pump it up and, of course, to add transmission fluid.

We didn't travel a hundred miles before another blowout. Of course, no longer did we have a spare. We got towed to another service station, where we bought two (mismatched, naturally) retread tires to replace this second blowout and the spare, which resumed its on-call status. And more transmission fluid. By now it seemed that we were pouring more transmission fluid into the car than gasoline.

We almost got through Massachusetts before yet another tire gave up the ghost, as it were.

Connecticut cost us two more tires. Always the cheapest we could find. At this point, all we wanted was to get home, where we could give the car away to some poor schmuck. Anybody.

Is it too much of a stretch for you to believe that we ended up replacing five tires in order to get me home? Well, it's God's own truth.

Phil drove me right to my door in Manhattan, like the obliging friend he was.

"How was the trip home?" my mother asked.

"It was OK."

Phil called me that evening to say, "I nearly made it."

"What do you mean, almost all the way to Bogota?"

"No. I nearly made it across the George Washington Bridge."

The last that was seen of the '56 Chevy Bel Air wagon was the junk man hauling it away from the right lane of the upper level of the George Washington Bridge. He got the vehicle, such as it was, for free.

Phil got a free lift to the junkyard in Fort Lee, where he was picked up by his father in a brand new 1967 Buick LeSabre, which his father never did let him drive.

A '56 Chevy BelAir wagon just like ours, only in considerably better shape, goes for $79,500 in today's market. Just saying.

There Cometh One Mightier

I left Astoria, Oregon, in 1983 and never went back. To be precise, I did go back, every year, sort of. If you count passing through on the way to Cannon Beach, then, yes, I did go back. However, I think going back should include stopping, at least for gas. Stopping at any of the five traffic lights is observing the law. You can't count that. Or can you? It depends upon how you look at it, I guess.

"You want to see something special?" This from a car repair shop technician in Rainier, Oregon, which is one-sixth the size of Astoria, meaning small. Very small. Rainier was still in its heyday, three years before the state's only nuclear power plant was shut down and then dismantled. As if it had never existed.

Rainier is another town that my family passed right through numerous times, usually without blinking. Right; you know where I am going with this: *Because if you blinked, you would miss it.* The Trojan power plant was tough to miss, but it didn't count, because it was outside of town. Where it needed to be. I mean, who would want to have a giant nuclear power plant in their back yard?

The Longview Bridge, which spans the Columbia River, terminates just outside of Rainier. I once rode my bicycle 150 miles from Seattle, yet, thirsty and tired as I was—facing another fifty miles before reaching the finish line of a race to Portland—I zipped past Rainier, with nary a nod to the good folks offering free water bottles.

This one day in 1991 was a different thing altogether.

The family was on its annual trek to Cannon Beach. There were six of us, five of whom were females. I was the token male. Everyone knows how women overpack. {I see male heads bobbing and females vehemently denying this incontrovertible fact.}

No surprise when I tell you that we needed two cars.

As usual, everybody wanted to be with Mom. Betsy, being five, and used to being coerced by her older sisters, was assigned to travel with me. The girls couldn't wait to get to our friend Tillie's house, where they could chase the ducks. Each girl would be allowed to pick a favorite and give it a name.

Each girl wanted to name her duck Erica for some inexplicable reason. So, there were four Ericas waiting to be chased at Tillie's, assuming the eagles, minks, or foxes didn't get to them first.

The big girls were pushing Mom to drive as fast as possible. Betsy and I followed behind in one of the nine or more Volvos that I have owned through the years. This particular Volvo tried to pull a fainting spell of sorts on the vast span of the Longview Bridge. Cellular memory of the '56 Chevy dying on the George Washington Bridge, only not quite as bad. Just major overheating and some disturbing loss of power.

Cars honking behind, even in sedate southern

Washington, we managed to limp over the hump and coast down to the Oregon side.

This reminded me of the time we were atop Mt. Haleakala at sunset, only to realize that we were out of gas. Betsy was with me then, too (also the same wife). My solution in both cases was the same, to coast downhill in neutral. In Maui, we coasted for 40 miles and rolled across the main drag to a gas station immediately opposite the turnoff to the mountain.

On this occasion, a mile or so in neutral sufficed to get us to Rainier. And (wonders will never cease) right there was a gas station, replete with service tech! I seem to have both good and bad luck with cars. Karma confusion.

"The radiator is shot."

"Can you fix it?"

"Oh sure. Only, we have to order the parts from Longview." I am relieved, because (a) the problem is fixable, and (b) the parts come from just on the other side of the bridge.

I, curiously: "How long do you think this will take?"

He, laconically (Remember, this is Rainier, Oregon.): "A few hours. Cute little girl you got there."

Betsy, sadly, holding back the tears: "My sisters will get to play with the ducks and they will chase Erica away before I get there." She was correct. The other car was long gone down the road, the rest of the family blissfully unaware of our plight. (These were the Dark Ages, before widespread use of cellular phones.)

I offered a cursory explanation to the tech, who said, "Aww," and patted Betsy on the head with a grimy hand.

"You hungry?" Silly question. 5-year-olds are always ready to eat. Just our luck; the snacks were in the other car.

Killing a few hours with a little kid in the outskirts of a small town can be challenging. I couldn't get her to nap, because she was all keyed up, so we took a walk on the side of the road and counted "slug bugs" (VW "beetles") as they motored by. With no restaurants or food markets in sight, I was praying that Betsy might forget that she was hungry.

We agreed that we would walk until we saw five "slug bugs" and then turn back. I took it as a good omen that the fifth one was gold (i.e., worth 400 points). Up ahead was a grocery store! Not quite miraculous, but a godsend, nonetheless.

"I'm hungry." Either of us could have said this by now.

Heading right for the cookies, Betsy suggested we take a bagful back to the garage for the nice man. So, we did.

He, with mouthful of cookie: "You want to see something special? Would your little girl like to see the World's Biggest Chainsaw?"

Betsy, innocently: "What's a chainsaw, Daddy?"

He brought us behind the garage, where sat the Mother of All Chainsaws. Betsy was not all that impressed, having no reference point for comparison. But I was bowled over: "Jesus, it's a behemoth!"

"Yup. 450 pounds. You think I am kidding? Here grab this handle." He whistled, and two other rather large, lumberjack-type fellows materialized. All four of us got in position, and, on the count of three, we lifted. Mercifully, the big boy on my side lifted quite a bit more than his share. My eyeballs were about to pop out.

I, barely able to get words out: "Okay. Can we put it down now?"

After I recovered, which took more than a little time and a more than a couple of cookies, I asked what in the world such a leviathan was used for. He told me they haul it around to logging festivals, about which I was supremely ignorant, even after living in Astoria for four years. (For the record, logging was about the only industry left in Astoria, once the last of the thirty-seven fish canneries had closed.)

"Yeah, well, they haul it over to a great big log, start the V-8 engine, heft it up, lay it on the log, and it cuts clean through in less than a second. God's own truth."

"Amen… That's it?"

"Yup, for that show. Then they pack it up, and off they go to another gig."

{You can look it up. Go to YouTube, where you can find everything that is, although not everything that ever was since the beginning, and look up "The Biggest, Longest, and Strongest CHAINSAW." It's right there. You will see several contest entries. But you will know which one I am telling you about, without a doubt.

You will be amazed, in part because these chainsaws are so monumental, in part because there are sizable gatherings (more than likely, near relatives) on hand to watch and cheer on their favorite team.}

He, eyes lighting up with distinct enthusiasm in his voice: "You want I should fire this baby up?" (Not really a baby at 450 lb., but okay.)

"Stand back. No, way back." There is a deafening roar, flames shooting up from the eight cylinders, heat radiating across the room. Betsy is impressed now.

"Can we do that again, Daddy?"

"NO!"

Actually, there is an even larger chainsaw. "Big Gus" is on display at Da Yoopers Tourist Trap, in Ishpeming, Michigan (four times the size of Rainier, at 6,000 souls). This phenom is six feet tall and twenty-two feet long. Too big to move. Also, too feeble to impress as a log cutter. It works, all right, but the motor that runs it is no V-8.

The main point about "Big Gus" is its entry in the *Guinness Book of World Records*.

Anyway, "Gus" was not made manifest until 1996. So, for all I know, the one we saw may well have been, at the time, the World's Largest Chainsaw.

The radiator was delivered and installed, thank God, and we moved on, driving right through Astoria, without stopping.

Moving Right Along

My first car, other than that other car, which really was only half my car, and anyway we let the junk man drive it away, come to think of it, was also driven away by the junk man. A different junk man, a different place, a different time…

Where was I?

My second first car had a stick shift. Stick shifts are hard to come by in new cars these days. But back then, you had to specify what you wanted. The car salesman would ask, "Are you looking to buy a manual or an automatic transmission?"

Manual transmission was the official terminology for what we, in common parlance, called a stick shift. Cool cats called it "four on the floor," although, if you count reverse, it really was five gears. And sometimes six.

Whatever.

My father had gone through a series of snazzy little sports cars during his male menopause—in turn, a Triumph, Lancia, and Sunbeam. As an adolescent, I enjoyed watching him rev the engine and pop the clutch to race the lights on Park Avenue, which he loved to do on early Sunday mornings, whenever weather conditions were right. Sadly, from my point of view, Dad recovered a measure of his perspective and switched to a Buick, with automatic transmission. And taught me how to drive it.

Although there was nothing sporty about the new Volvo that Mom bought for me, I did opt for a stick shift to jazz it up a bit.

The check was written, the car—first in a long line of Volvos that I was to own—was delivered to the dealership, and I got the call to come and get it. Which I did. Except that I didn't know how to operate a clutch. Or how to move the gear shift. In New York City, as I recall on 96th St., two blocks from the East River.

The Volvo dealership had no space in their lot for practicing. The salesman had no interest in teaching me how to drive my new car. It was sink or swim, so to speak.

The car was beautiful, but my initial attempts to drive it were anything but. I must have stalled ten times just trying to get it out of the lot. Only three or four more times in traffic, mostly coming out of red lights. Somehow, I got that car downtown and into the neighborhood garage intact.

Comparatively speaking, things went reasonably well after that. I actually got fairly proficient at driving a shift. Well, I did have to have the clutch replaced once or twice. But who's counting?

I drove that car all over the Northeast during my senior year in college and kept it through medical school in New York City. Parked it on the street and only got a few tickets, as opposed to my classmate from Wyoming, who amassed a whopping $3,500 in parking tickets. Never paid a dime, as he knew that in those pre-computer days, there was no reciprocity between New York and Wyoming.

Anyway, one day, with a bit of spare time between Pharmacology and Biochemistry exams, I thought, *This will be the perfect time to teach my girlfriend how to drive a stick shift.*

"I don't want to do that."

"Why not?"

"Because you will yell at me."

"What makes you think so?"

"Because my father started yelling at me when he tried to teach me how to drive a stick shift."

Here was my chance to really prove my worth as a boyfriend. "I won't yell at you."

And I didn't. For at least four minutes. Probably trying to teach her to use a clutch on a steep hill was a bad idea. Maybe, come to think of it, the whole thing was a bad idea. Because she never managed to get the car out of the parking space.

In fairness, she was yelling at me, too. So, maybe I was simply yelling back.

A little old lady was walking by, pulling her grocery cart behind her, stockings rolled at the top of her calves. My girlfriend, having totally lost it by now, got out of the car, part-way out of the parking spot, slammed the door, looked at this total stranger, and yelled, in a complete non sequitur, "Would you let this maniac take your gall bladder out?"

The woman, trying to mind her own business on the mean streets of New York, sized up the situation, said nothing, and took off, as fast as her rolled-up-stockinged legs would carry her.

To be absolutely clear, at that point in time I hadn't taken out anybody's gallbladder. Nor had I observed any gallbladder surgery. The comment perhaps was prescient, though a bit premature. I tried to explain all of this to my girlfriend. No success, either about my ignorance of gall bladder surgery, or at teaching her to drive a shift.

We broke up after that. Actually twice. More about this later.

I wasn't going to let my daughters grow up steeped in such ineptitude. I was determined that they would learn how to drive a stick shift. My first Volvo was long gone, thanks to junk man number two, but I replaced it with another stick shift car. I bought this, knowing that my wife would never be able to drive it. I knew better than to try to teach her.

My daughters were a different story. I reasoned, *Suppose they are on a date, and their boyfriend is suddenly incapacitated?* (It has been known to happen.) *What if they are in a stick shift car?? Imagine they are out in the middle of nowhere???* Cell phones were just becoming the thing, but only CEOs and MDs carried these big brick-like things around.

I started with my oldest. Fortuitously, she is the most coordinated. We practiced in a nearby vacant parking lot, where she got the hang of it reasonably quickly. As a result, I bought her an extremely-used, manual transmission Volvo, which she handled very well, considering the creakiness of the vehicle, until the rear axle fell off. Junk man number three took care of that.

The second oldest presented some problems, including significantly less hand/eye coordination and an attitude. I took her to that same parking lot on a Sunday morning, turned the car over to her, lovingly tried to coach her, soon began yelling at her, and watched her walk home, muttering to herself, completely deflated. I bought her an automatic transmission Volvo, pretty much of a has-been, which lasted almost a year, before it was totaled and towed away. I must have some weird affinity for junk men.

By now, my second manual transmission car was history, and my wife wouldn't consider letting me buy anything that wasn't automatic. So even trying to teach the youngest two daughters to use a clutch was no longer an option. I simply told them never to date a boy driving a stick shift car.

Flash forward. I am back with my old girlfriend. This time for good. Before she agreed to return for one more try, she only had one question: "What kind of car do you drive these days?"

"Don't worry."

Okay then. She is back. We enjoy a blissful, happy

marriage. Practically nothing to yell about. We plan a trip to England.

I am no fool. I know that driving is wrong sided in the UK. Still, I believe I can manage it. After all, I am a surgeon, used to looking at an overhead monitor to do laparoscopic surgery. How hard can it be to drive on the wrong side of the road? I get myself an International Driver's License, just in case, because you never know.

There is no way that I will drive a car in London. Salisbury is another thing. We make plans to travel by train to Salisbury and pick up a rental car there. Then motor to Stonehenge and on from there to the Cotswolds, Bath, and eastern Wales.

The clerk at AAA had found me a sweet deal in Salisbury—a car with automatic transmission. My thinking was, *It will be challenging enough to drive on the wrong side without also having to fiddle with a clutch and gear shift.*

I leave my wife in the parking lot of the train station. These are modern times now, and I have a cell phone, complete with international minutes. We only take one phone, since we plan always to stick together. I find the exact location of the Eurocar place, using Google Maps.

"This won't take long, honey. You stay there with the bags."

The place turns out to be about twice as far away as I thought, but still at a walkable distance.

"Is my car ready?"

"Sorry. We do not have an automatic at this moment."

"When will you have one?"

"I am hoping in about four hours. Will that be satisfactory"

This will not work, because we have an appointment to visit Stonehenge in two hours. {Oh yes, you need an appointment now. And you cannot get walk amidst the stones. Forget the good old days. They are long gone. Can't be too careful anymore, right? Suppose a stone were to fall over on someone?}

"We do have a manual transmission vehicle available now." Okay, so you know that I can drive a stick shift car. But I am mired in a major quandary, *CAN I DO THIS, FROM THE WRONG SIDE OF THE VEHICLE, ON THE WRONG SIDE OF THE ROAD?*

The agent interrupts my thought processes to say, "I believe that Enterprise has automatic vehicles available."

Things may be looking up. "Is the place nearby?"

"Oh yes, sir. Just up the road a bit. A bit was quite a bit more than I was led to believe. But hope springs eternal, so off I went.

I inquire, "Would you happen to have an automatic car available?"

He looks at me like I am from some remote climate, which I am, relative to his fog-laden, drizzly locale.

"No, sir, I do not. But I have a manual transmission vehicle available now." *Is this a broken record? Am I in the Twilight Zone, or Salisbury?* I am getting desperate.

"How much?" He quotes a price exactly twice as high as my AAA contract with Eurocar.

So, back I trudge to Eurocar, thinking, *My wife must be getting worried now, all blue and forlorn in the train station parking lot, surrounded by suitcases and possibly suspicious strangers.* I am wishing I could call her, but—well, you know…

I get back to the first place, now finding four customers ahead of me, and only the one agent. They are all speaking together in some Eastern European language. I think, *It could be worse*, being generally an optimist when it comes to situations like this. I mean, *How long can it take to fix up this Slavic horde with a car?*

Actually, it takes quite a while, because they are resorting all too frequently to their pocket English/something-Slavic manual of handy phrases. And they have brought out a sort of crude calculator over which they seemed to be arguing.

Finally, they come both to an understanding and an agreement, and leave the counter, rental car keys in hand, looking as happy as Slavs can look.

"I am back, and now I would like to rent that manual transmission car."

"Terribly sorry. We do not have one ready just now. The party ahead of you took the one I offered you earlier." He sees tears welling in my eyes, and offers, "I can have one ready for you in a quarter hour. It's actually a lovely Vauxhall, for which we ordinarily charge more than the car you were expecting to get. I will give it you (Do I care if he left off the "to" at this point?) for the contract price."

I reach across the counter to try to hug the man. This is well before COVID social distancing, but the British never have understood such spontaneity. "Thank you, sir, but a hug is not necessary."

Driving on the wrong side is quite unsettling. For one thing, the steering wheel is on the right. So are the pedals, obviously. When you look up at the rearview mirror, it isn't where you expect it to be. Taking your first right from a two-way street into another two-way street is an adventure. Yet, that is nothing compared with the horror of attempting to go into, and hopefully out of, a roundabout the wrong way, which is the right way for these backward people.

Add to this, having to operate a clutch and a stick shift with the wrong hand and foot. Disorienting is a word that pops into the old noggin.

I manage to pull out of the Eurocar lot without unduly embarrassing myself in front of the more-than-somewhat-bemused agent. Stalling only three times is a considerable improvement over what happened the first time I attempted to drive a shift, in the Volvo car lot.

Keeping in mind, as best I can, the lawful side of the road, I make it back to the train station. Nobody ever has been happier to see me than my wife, at that moment. I have been gone over an hour and a half.

"Are you driving a stick shift? I thought we were getting an automatic."

"Long story. But don't worry. I can handle this."

On our way to Stonehenge, unaware of the exact whereabouts of the left side of the car, I will admit to shading a bit too far to the left, as these giant lorries (i.e., trucks—the English make up odd names for common things, like "loo") come rumbling by. Fortunately, we are in the countryside. Disrupting the hedgerows is better for the car, and for us, than hitting a cement curb.

I am too terrified and focused on trying to drive to look over at my wife, who is too terrified to speak. I pray that, after a few slight mishaps, I will have it down.

I know that this would be a bad time to joke about her giving it a try. (And I also know by now how to safely remove a gallbladder.)

Several years later, I am traveling with my youngest daughter and boyfriend in Scotland. She has made all the car rental arrangements and has an iron-clad guarantee of an automatic to pick up in Edinburgh.

"I will do the driving, honey. I managed before, and it wasn't easy." The boyfriend is in agreement, my daughter slightly miffed.

The automatic lessens the terror of driving on the wrong side of the road a bit. Thing is, there are these roundabouts everywhere. Just when your blood pressure is reverting to normal, up comes another one. It's almost more than a person can take!

{Wrong-way roundabouts are the way the English get back at us for dumping their tea into Boston harbor.}

Somewhere in the middle of the Highlands, where there are more sheep than cars, going through a small village, I relent and let my daughter have a go at driving. Two and a half minutes later, a lorry comes rumbling by, and, Bingo! We are up on the curb and halfway onto the sidewalk.

Everyone is yelling. My daughter is yelling about lorries coming out of nowhere and frightening her. Her boyfriend, thrown sideways in the back, is yelling that she has scared the shit out of him (hyperbole, thank God), and I am yelling at her to stop the car and let me take over the wheel. Which she does. And I do.

All of this gives new perspective to the Beatles' song, "Drive My Car":

Baby, you can drive my car (when we get back to the States). *Yes, I'm going to be a star* (because I didn't harm any persons or vehicles). *Baby, you can drive my car* (as long as it is an automatic), *And maybe I'll love you* (if you do not yell at lorries or frighten any little old ladies).

Beep, beep, beep, beep, YEAH!

The Downside of Pedagogy

I really do love to teach. The highest praise I ever received from my surgical mentors was that I was a good teacher. They might have come to the conclusion that I was a good surgeon, too, had I scrupulously followed the party line. Thing is, I was taught all the way through college to think independently. Medical school and surgical residency were more about regurgitation of facts and never daring to divert from the party line. I did what I had to do (mostly), but this required a totally different mindset, and I never was willing to commit totally to such a mental makeover.

I did learn along the way never to say no to any referral or any remotely reasonable request.

"Will you please teach me to drive?" This not from one of my children, but from a forty-something-year-old friend.

Requests such as this must be as rare as hens' teeth.

Chi-min is a dear friend, and Mary and I had been witnesses at his wedding to Hortense some years previously. He is an engineer, and she a French opera singer and vocal coach. We commiserated with their visa hassles, attended recitals and annual student productions of *Faust*, even celebrated Chinese New Year together.

Last thing I knew, they were using public transportation and the occasional Uber to get around town.

"No longer. We bought a car! I have a learner's permit."

"Does Hortense have a driver's license?" He nods affirmatively.

"So, why can't she teach you?"

"Because she gets nervous and yells at me."

Have you ever been yelled at by an opera singer? A nervous one?? In close quarters??? I take his point.

"What about a driver's ed program?" He tells me he completed one.

"Well, if you already did that, why do you need me?"

Chi-min is intelligent. He has several advanced degrees and is very precise in what he does. We witnessed this firsthand in the meticulous way he performed the Chinese New Year tea ceremony.

"I just don't think I learned enough in the twelve classes to be a good driver."

Now please understand that I am not one to racially profile. Although everybody in New York knows that New Jersey and Massachusetts drivers of all races, gender associations, and ethnic types are atrocious drivers, some would have it that Asian drivers are a bit further under par. Sexist types, not me you understand, would go on to say that female Asian drivers are the worst. Clearly, they have not driven through traffic circles in or around Boston, where indiscriminate ineptitude is pervasive among virtually all who attempt to pass through unscathed.

Anyway, as I mentioned, Chi-min is a friend, and do not forget that I was trained as a surgical resident to accept all cases, no matter how much of a Friday afternoon dump they might have appeared to be. Besides, this was a Wednesday.

"Okay. When do you want to start?"

"How would tomorrow afternoon be?" *This man obviously is raring to go.*

Thursday afternoon, I drive over to his neighborhood, over the rather vehement objections of my dear wife, who insists on offering a variety of unsolicited suggestions, such as, "Why can't he practice with Hortense? A pair of ear plugs, and he would be fine."

Mind you, Mary uses ear plugs every night, and oftentimes during the day. Her beautifully-formed ears have subtly adapted to the near-constant use of ear plugs, which fit in her outer canals as if they were bespoke, specifically to filter out much or most of what I may be trying to speak about, especially baseball.

Only once did she manage to get one ear plug wedged in, to the point where she could not remove it and had to find an ENT surgeon in New York City to fish it out. Two minutes/ $550. Had I been with her at the time, I would have taken care of the problem for free. The way I took care of my then four-year-old daughter, Katie, the day she got a crayon stub stuck in her nose.

Getting back to the subject at hand, I see Chi-min

waiting for me precisely at the appointed hour, a big grin on his face, as he points to his proud purchase, a practically moribund Chevy Impala from the last century.

"Nice car, Chi-min," thinking, *Kind of smells like my exceedingly-used '56 BelAir that barely lasted eight weeks before giving up the ghost...*

"Wait until I open the passenger side door from the inside. Oh, and you cannot roll the window down on your side."

"How much did you pay for this car?"

"$500. That was cheap, don't you think?" I simply can't offer an opinion, which is just as well, being flooded with memories, thinking back to 1965, *When you could buy a beater for fifty dollars, abandon it when it ceased to function right smack in the middle of the George Washington Bridge, and have the junk man haul it away and your father come get you...*

Snapping out of my reverie, "So, what do you feel you need to practice first?"

"Everything."

I am really glad that Mary is praying for me. She frequently does, but I am thinking, *I need prayer more than ever right about now.* Also, that, *If I get home safely, I will call her cousin the priest and ask for a little extra consideration from him as well.*

I suggest that we start out with an assessment of Chi-min's parallel parking skills—sort of like medical schools using gross anatomy right from the get-go to weed out those who are unfit. This is a mistake. I soon find out that, although he isn't completely inept at steering the car in a forward direction, going backwards is, at best, a crap shoot.

I have him give it a go, and he barely scrapes the rear street-side bumper of the car in front on the sixteenth or seventeenth try. Immediately, a rather irate man appears.

"What the hell are you doing?" Or words to that matter. I think, *We must have attracted his attention, much like that of a dozen or so other neighbors, fascinated, in a* schadenfreude *way, by Chi-min's futile attempts to parallel park.*

"I just got my car (a late-model, shiny Audi, as unlike Chi-min's car as Medusa to Aphrodite) back from the shop yesterday. I was having this same bumper repaired, damn it."

I ask Chi-min if he had been practicing with Hortense a week or two earlier. Since he assures me that he had not, I feel reasonably confident that, *We only are responsible for the present ding.*

"Do you have insurance? Yes? Well, give this nice man the information."

The "nice man" takes what he needs and walks off, muttering unmentionables.

"Let's quit for the day," I say, hopefully.

"Oh no, I am fine. I have another hour. Let's drive somewhere," he says, ebulliently.

Out of luck, off we go. Chi-min is driving down the middle of a two-way street. After several reminders, a few angry looks, and more honks than one is accustomed to hearing in a residential Seattle neighborhood, he does move over, to the point of relocating a couple of bushes a bit more than somewhat.

He swerves to avoid a young mother pushing a stroller, attempting to cross at a well-marked crosswalk.

"You saw that mother and baby, right? Why didn't you stop for them?"

"Because I could see that I could get through without hitting them."

"And what about that stop sign?"

"What stop sign?"

"Maybe I should drive us back now and park the car."

"Why? Don't you think I am doing okay?"

I am too busy praying to answer.

We try a few right-hand turns, and they go reasonably well. Left-hand turns not so good, but better with time. I muster the courage to guide him through a few neighborhood traffic circles. He gets the right-hand turn, but he requires some patient explanation to negotiate properly to the left. He leaves a divot in the curb and the center circle on the same attempt. (This is not easy to do, even if one were to set out with that goal in mind.)

Somehow we manage to make it back to the starting point. Mercifully, I see a spot that Chi-min can glide into straight ahead. The car he scraped is gone—parked somewhere as far away as is practicable, I suspect.

I stagger back to the safe confines of my car. Chi-min follows. "Thank you so much! And thank you for not yelling at me. You are such a good teacher! Will next week at the same time work for you?"

I really need to say, *No time will,* but I fall back to my surgical residency default position. "Oh, sure. See you then."

"Are you kidding me?" Mary wants me to call immediately and retract my agreement.

"Tell him anything. Tell him you are going in for a heart transplant."

I cannot tell a lie. Instead, I borrow three construction cones and head over to meet Chi-min with a fail-safe plan. I will use cones and the curb on a deserted street for parallel parking practice. On the way to this remote spot, we pass four stop signs, and Chi-min actually observes three—well, two and a half, because he is halfway into the intersection past the first one before he remembers to come to a complete stop.

We work on parallel parking for the better part of an hour. We ruin two of the three cones and scrape both wheel rims of the right side of the Impala. Not that you could see much difference, really.

Then we spend another fifteen minutes practicing backing around the corner. "Will they examine me on this skill (*Or lack thereof,* I think, rather uncharitably)?"

I know they will not, but I am afraid to have him drive down any streets that are populated with anything other than wildlife, and I am trying to use up all our allotted time.

"In three days, I have a conference in Bellevue."

"Are you going to ride over there with one of your colleagues?"

"No. I think I will drive." He appears to be serious. I think, *I might be getting carsick.*

"But this means freeway driving. Are you sure you can do this? And will there be someone with you who has a driver's license?"

"I think I will be okay. I will drive very carefully. My assistant will be with me." *Not for much longer*, I am thinking.

THIS IS NOT OKAY. I fear for all the unsuspecting drivers out there, whether or not they have been baptized.

"I think we need to practice a bit more. Tell you what, let's have you try a little freeway driving." I now realize, to my utter dismay, that, *I am a responsible person who, despite the best of intentions, may now be responsible for creating an unparalleled road hazard.*

And off we go. I have him enter Interstate 5, which he does, barely.

"Move over one lane. Look in your rearview mirror first." He doesn't appear to know where that is. I show him.

"But don't keep staring at it. Keep your eyes on the road."

"How am I supposed to look in the rearview mirror (which he now has successfully identified) and also keep my eyes on the road?"

Jesus H. Christ, I think. Since he might be a Buddhist, perhaps I should say, as serenely as possible, *Didn't they teach you anything at the driving school about the route cause of unnecessary suffering?* (At least, my facility at punning is still operational.) But what I actually say is, "You cast a quick glance at the mirror. And not just once...repeatedly."

We move on to the sideview mirrors. These he knows about. At least, he knows where they are. Knowing how and when to use them is another thing. And then there is the windshield wiper. And the turn indicator signal control. This whole thing is a kind of magical mystery tour.

We are still in the same far-right lane, after all that, with a left-sided exit coming up soon.

Now I am praying again, *Father, guide him, for he knows not what he does.* Thanks be to God; I get him off the highway.

"That was fun!"

Maybe for you. I check to make sure my pants are still dry; my armpits certainly are not.

"I can't make it next week." I need extra time to recover from this session. "Call me when (*if?*) you get home from the conference." In a perverse way that I am not proud of, I need to hear how it goes.

It manages to go, and we continue to practice. Week after week. I must admit that he is improving. How could he not, considering the point from which he started? Even parallel parking is almost acceptable, 33% of the time. Diagonal parking needs a few more years' work.

"I think I am ready now to take my test." I don't necessarily agree, but these driving lessens are wearing Mary's hands raw from all the wringing, praying and whatnot.

"Tell you what, I will give you a driving test myself first."

I show up, checklist in hand, playing the role of examiner to the hilt. All seriousness, no playful banter, not so much as a "How're things going?" Just the business at hand. After all, my reputation as a volunteer supplemental driving instructor for insecure middle-aged Asian men is on the line.

"Turn on the car." (*Seatbelts? Adjust mirrors?*) "Pull out into the street." (*Blinkers? Use of rearview and side mirrors?*) "Drive straight ahead." (*Correct side of road? Observe that stop sign?*) "Park on your right up ahead." (*Within six inches of the curb? Maximum four maneuvers?*)

I really put him through the wringer.

While I cannot say he passes, because he forgets to signal before a left-hand turn, and it takes him six maneuvers to park, I cannot handle any more lessons.

"Good luck. Let me know how it goes (*the first few times you try to pass*)."

"I PASSED!" Wonders will never cease. "Hortense and I would like to take you and Mary out to dinner to celebrate."

"Congratulations. Where you do you want to meet for dinner?"

"At the Thai restaurant in Wallingford. We will stop by and pick you up. I will drive."

"That's okay. We'll take our own car."

II. Near and Dear

À *La Recherche des Choses Perdues*

{Literally "in search of lost things"}

School mugs, banners, and other rah-rah stuff often lose their pride of place to other items we accumulate as time passes. They are relegated to plastic bins, boxes, or trunks with other keepsakes—maybe in the back of a closet, maybe in the attic, maybe in a storage unit. After a while, we tend to forget where. Which sometimes makes rummaging through random stuff a delightful and surprising adventure. You never know what you might find.

One day, some forty-five years after graduating from college, during the process of downsizing, I came across my college mug. As I cleaned it up in preparation for filling it up with a cold beer for old times' sake, I noticed that in fact it wasn't my mug at all. It had my roommate's nickname on it. I considered calling him up to inquire whether he had mine, secondary to a swap, intentional or inadvertent as it may have been.

I resisted this temptation, because I feared that he (a) might have lost or broken mine, (b) couldn't locate it at the moment, or (c) never had it in the first place. And then where would I be? More than likely, he would want his back, and I would be bereft of a perfectly useful college mug that I might have wanted to use again before forgetting where I put it. The fact that I hardly ever drink beer anymore is irrelevant.

Sometimes you hear about something that you haven't thought about for so long that it almost seems like it must have been part of someone else's life. Just the other day, for example, an old girlfriend FB messaged me about six spoons from the 1960 Olympics that she claims I gave her. She can't remember where she put them, but told me that, "if they ever show up again," she will send them back to me. Thing is, I cannot remember ever having given them to her. Or ever having them in my own possession. Or ever having seen them at all.

This is not to say that I wasn't there in Rome for the 1960 Olympics. I was, and I certainly remember that well. I remember my brother dragging me off to every swimming event, three times a day, for over a week. Then all the water polo matches. And then most of the track and field events. In those days, tickets were readily available and surprisingly affordable.

Please do not misunderstand. It was a thrill to be there. Mother brought me, a twelve-year-old, and my big brother, who had trained for a bid to make the US swim team, only to damage his knee and miss Olympic trials. Mom was smarter than to venture out thrice daily to the swimming venue through all the summer heat. She limited herself to finals, always held in the evening, and always when the outside temperature was significantly cooler.

Picture me, a skinny little kid, at Olympic events all day long and into the late evening—in our spare time walking through the Olympic village with my brother, who was on a first-name basis with so many of the swimmers, even those from as far away as Australia and Japan. We were busily trading pins with the athletes at every opportunity. I can't remember ever stopping to eat so much as a single plate of pasta, which might explain why I lost ten pounds over the two-week time period.

We came home laden with scads of pins from just about everywhere. My brother had them mounted and framed and to this day has them hanging in his house, along with his medals from AAU national championships and from his long career in national security. Walls full of pins and medals. But, like the illusory food, I cannot recall seeing any Olympic spoons in Rome, back home in New York, or in my brother's trophy room.

Perhaps my old girlfriend got the six 1960 Rome Olympics souvenir spoons from someone else. Perhaps my brother had a stash of them somewhere, took a liking to the girl, and passed them off to her without telling me. She did say that she hung out with him after we had broken up, which is a bit awkward and something that he denies.

At this point, to paraphrase Hillary Clinton, does it really matter?

Then there is the matter of my class ring. Unlike the chimerical spoons and my roomie's mug, I cared a lot about this ring. I kept it in a special place in my desk drawer and would pull it out and wear it on special occasions. My parents had bought it for me at the end of sophomore year, when they were reasonably sure that I was more likely than not to graduate.

I wore it to weddings. I wore it to opening nights at the opera, to reunions, to a few funerals. I wore it whenever I put on formal wear. I wore it to important interviews. I wore it on television, when I was interviewed about weight loss surgery.

And, just like that, I lost it. Well, not really lost it. It was stolen, and not from the safe place where I had kept it for years, but from the glove compartment of my youngest daughter's car. She had it there for a number of months after I had split the sheets with her mother, leaving it and a number of other things of mine behind. Her intent was always to give the ring back to me on some special occasion. Sadly, a car prowler presented himself in advance of that occasion.

Rather than tell me about the theft, she turned repeatedly to eBay, hoping to find a 1970 Yale ring offered for sale. After some months and many frustrating internet searches, she spilled the beans.

"I have something to confess, Dad."

Immediately, I was reminded of the last time she said this, when she was seventeen.

That was two years after having her belly button pierced, contrary to the rules set up by my ex and myself: one piercing to each ear, max, per daughter—not before age eighteen; and no tattoos before twenty-one—preferably never.

She had chosen to tell us, one parent at a time, after we had divorced. She took her mother into confidence, after first making her promise that she would not get angry or tell me. Shortly thereafter, on Father's Day, she fessed up to me.

I took this second blockbuster revelation in stride, more or less. We were in a queue at a book signing event, where I had to be measured in my response. Yet, the more I thought about this in the ensuing days, the more upset I became.

Googling the company that had made my ring, I found, to my dismay, that style to have been discontinued and the mold destroyed in favor of a "more modern," sleeker look.

I, too, resorted to eBay, despite all odds, typing in the search box "Yale ring." What a shock! Lo and behold, there was a Yale ring for sale, exactly like mine, except that the date was 1973. And in seemingly good shape, other than a full-thickness crack across the bottom.

I contacted the seller to ascertain the provenance of the piece. He told me that he had found it on the beach, in Tel Aviv. This seemed a bit sketchy. I conjured up images of foul play: pirates, assassins, car prowlers, or a mini Arab-Israeli uprising. At the same time, I reminded myself that there are no coincidences and showed photos of the ring to a jeweler.

"Any chance you can make this three into a zero?" To my eye, it looked like it could be done. "And how about the break in the back? Can that be fixed?"

"Yes, but it will cost you. What does this guy want for the ring?"

I told him. He raised his eyebrows. "For a ten-karat ring? That's quite a bit."

I indicated how desperate I was to buy it, especially now that he told me he could perform the necessary alteration and repair. "It's not the gold that makes it valuable, it's the nostalgia, and the fact that old Yale rings never seem to come onto the market. I think all the old Yalies must take them to their graves."

This was a bridge too far for the jeweler, but he humored me. After all, a job like this helps pay the rent.

So, I bought the ring, prayed that it would arrive safe and partly sound from Israel. And, sure enough, it made it through customs and to my mailbox. Two weeks later, I had what, for all intents and purposes, looked just like my old ring.

Astonishingly, I happened to peruse eBay as I took a break from writing this vignette and found, not one, but two more Yale rings like mine—only they were from '55 and '69. Even my jeweler would balk at trying to alter either of those dates to '70. I got lucky on the first try.

Now, if only the pandemic would end—with me surviving—so that I could find some reason to get all spiffed up again. And put on my new old Yale ring. Assuming that I remember where I put it. I'm sure it's someplace around here. Someplace safe. Not in the spoon drawer. After all, you never know whether a prowler might come snooping after silverware.

Gilda

The second redo of life together for Mary and me began in Seattle's quirkiest neighborhood. Fremont is renowned for, among other things: nude bicyclists, prominently displaying themselves at the summer solstice parade; a for-sale, monumental statue of Vladimir Lenin, specially decorated each year for Christmas; a rocket, complete with neon lights and on-demand clouds of ersatz fuel exhaust; the former—if not possibly-still-functioning—practice studio for Pearl Jam; a giant troll under the Aurora Bridge, in the process of devouring a VW Beetle; an obligatory authenticated chunk of the Berlin Wall; a sculpture of a family of four plus their dog, entitled "Waiting for the Interurban," which has never and likely will never stop there; and an outdoor Sunday market.

Much of our furnishings came either from the Fremont Sunday Market or from appropriated discards found in the trash room (down the hall from our apartment), which I frequently would check out—early in the day, so as to get first dibs. Pickings were plentiful, I assure you, because it seemed like someone was either moving in or moving out every day. And we, too, ended up moving out after some time—giving away almost all of the above.

But back in the beginning of our second reset, we found ourselves in need of a coat rack.

Which is what led us to Gilda, whom we found at

the Sunday market, naked and forlorn—actually in five pieces. It was enough to make two grown people cry.

"What are you selling her for?"

"How much of her do you want?"

"What do you mean?"

"Well, you can have the stand for five bucks…"

"Why would we want just the stand?"

"I dunno. Maybe you have another mannequin lying around."

"Actually, no. We might be interested in the rest of her."

"Okay. Well, the arms are eight bucks apiece; the torso, with the head, by the way, because I can't pull them apart, is twenty bucks; the legs, which also have to stay together, go for fifteen. You can always saw them apart later, if you want to."

"So, that would make forty-eight dollars for all of her, including the stand?"

"No, but I can let you have the whole thing for fifty."

"But that doesn't add up!"

"She has this wig here. Without her wig, she would be bald."

We had enough cash to buy either the mannequin or a moderately-priced coat rack. Although we traversed the market thoroughly, there wasn't a coat rack to be had.

Always thinking ahead, I suggested, "If we buy this mannequin, we could dress her up with multiple layers of coats. Maybe we wouldn't need a coat rack."

"What a great idea, honey!" I think she said that

because we were still in the honeymoon period, as it were, trying to make things work out for a third time. Mary doesn't know much about baseball, but she does know the adage "Three strikes, and you're out." Everyone knows that.

"If these parts don't fit together, will you refund our money?"

"Trust me, they fit. I put her together and take her apart all the time. And tell you what, you can have her for forty-eight bucks. I'll throw the wig in for free."

We took Gilda, which the man said was her given name, home with us, fully rearticulated, and set her up in the living room, adjacent to the balcony. Mary freshened her lipstick and nail polish, repairing a few chips here and there. Gilda lived with us, always clothed to excess, and always in out-of-season styles, for ten years. During that time, she acquired some items that remained all her own: Seattle SuperSonics underwear, a feathered boa, and several wigs in bold colors.

There must have been something about her which frightened the hummingbirds, because nary a one was inclined to visit the feeder suspended over the balcony until the day she was reluctantly given away, in preparation for vacating the apartment. That very day, a hummingbird actually flew into our living room, doubtless to ascertain whether Gilda was really gone.

Gilda now resides at Judy's Alterations, in Fremont, half a block from The Center of the Known Universe, which features directions to Xanadu, in case you have lost your way. She is resplendently attired in a lovely wedding dress, waiting patiently for Mr. Right to come along. We have full and unrestricted visitation rights, Tuesdays through Saturdays, 9-5. Judy promised that we could take her back when she retires, wedding dress not included.

Baby, It's Cold Inside

Our floating home was built around 1913. That was the year Woodrow Wilson succeeded William Howard Taft as President, relieving the nation of the somewhat overinflated fear of an oversized President getting stuck in the White House bathtub.

There is no chance of that happening to either one of us. Neither of us is overweight, nor do we live in a white house. Nor do we have a bathtub, for that matter, even after renovating our floating home, which originally had what one of our neighbors referred to as a "one butt" bathroom.

"That's exactly what it is," I replied. "But how did you know? Have you actually ever tried to answer the call of nature in it?"

"Naturally. We used to live in your place. By the way, how are you managing with that bed? What about the old sofa?"

It turns out that they were not the only ones to have lived in our new place—in fact, most of the community had, at one time or another, called it home. No one stuck it out for more than a couple of years.

Sometime in the remote past, two of the more intrepid of the multitudes who unsuccessfully had tried to make this floating home more livable added a second floor.

The obvious advantage of increased living space partly compensated for the increased hazard of capsizing. This clear and present danger was mollified somewhat by appropriating an errant, still-buoyant cedar log and affixing it, however tenuously, to the float—the legality of which has yet to be challenged in court.

Our involvement began with an offhand remark: "I am thinking about selling my Lake Union floating home," or words to that effect from a supine postoperative patient. *I am not thinking about buying a floating home* is what I was thinking, as I inspected her gastric bypass surgical scar. We were living in a perfectly capacious two-bedroom, two-bathroom flat in the funky Fremont section of Seattle. Alas, bathing was out of the question, because my wife had repurposed the tub as an extra closet.

"Why don't you go visit your brother in Cabo for a while?" I had never been to Mexico, and, since the opportunity presented itself, I concurred and went.

"So, what do you want to do today, Jimmy?" My brother is thinking that I will want to head right for the beach and do some whale watching.

"If you don't mind, I think I will take a bath."

On return, I asked Mary, mostly in jest, what she thought about taking a flier and living on the water.

"Like in a sailboat? You know I hate to get wet," this from a former lifeguard, who had since put away childish things and no longer had a swimsuit to her name. Which perhaps explains why Mary had no problem sacrificing our Fremont apartment bathtub.

"We are not going to Maui unless you buy yourself a swimsuit!" My brother had offered us a free week in his time share (complete with bathtub).

I dragged Mary to a swimwear store, where she proceeded to set an all-time record. She walked in, tried on two bikinis, bought one and left within the space of nine minutes. Gave her bikini to Goodwill three days after returning from Hawaii. And agreed to take a look at what my patient was thinking about selling, when I explained that I was told it was a house sitting on a raft and securely moored to a dock.

Perry Como was right: "The bluest skies you'll ever see are in Seattle." He didn't qualify his claim by admitting that, more often than not, the sky is gray. That certainly was the case, the day we drove over to take a look. The color above was mimicked by the wall coloring, not to mention the formerly-white, mammoth leather sofa, which, like the shag rug, now featured variegated shades and stains of gray.

Charming in an inscrutable way, but not our cup of tea—that was our feeling. Only we never really came out and said the second part. Not a couple to rush into things, we said nothing further to each other, to the kids, or anyone. Which was fine with my patient, the owner, because she it turned out that she was ambivalent about selling anyway.

Louise had a government job and used the home as her office, placing numerous heavy file cabinets on the second floor. The resulting top-heaviness, plus her weight, made the home more unstable, despite the purloined log. The high winds of late November were what made her more serious about selling. This would have to be done privately, as there was little or no chance of the building passing code.

Per co-op tradition, any home to be sold should first be offered to the community. On the other hand, since nearly everyone already had tried living there and knew the downside risks involved, any consideration of snapping it up before outsiders could have a go inspired either no reaction or snickering. Along came we two for a second look, now thinking that maybe the place could serve as a second home, a weekend retreat, or a cozy nest for our out-of-town friends. After a bit of back-and-forth negotiating, we settled on a price.

"…And you can keep the nice leather couch in the living room."

"Thank you," we told the seller—politely, because my wife is a leading authority on etiquette, and naively, because we figured that what had been brought in must be removable. That is, until we took measurements.

That was one major issue. The "one butt" bathroom was another. Not only was there no room for a bathtub; the shower was diminutive (Read: RV size). And the shame that accompanied that realization—more than the impossibility of removing the monstrous sofa, the tendency to tilt, or the challenges posed by a bed that could only be accessed from one side—was what led us to spend three years renovating the place.

For starters, we thought we should brighten it up. We hired a pre-med, part-time barista to repaint the interior in colors selected by an artist friend.

"That old couch is kind of gross. It's got to go," he opined, out of the blue.

"Unfortunately, it can't be dislodged. I measured it, the narrow stairway, and the doors. Even if we could somehow get it out the door and onto the porch, it is far too heavy to lower over the balcony to the dock. They must have built that second floor around the sofa!"

"No worries. My friend has a chain saw." And so, out it went. In four pieces.

Next, we installed the artist for a week to paint murals, giving her carte blanche, which is what you must do with an artist who is your friend, if you hope to maintain the relationship. Her solution to the bathroom was to expand it with huge floor-to-ceiling vistas of a jungle, replete with leopards, a frog, a toucan or three, a river, dense forestation, and a sky above—the paragon of panoramic "one butt" bathrooms.

She put a cloudy-sky ceiling on the second floor. We asked for a gaggle of geese on the wing, a float plane, and a blue bird as well. She got a bit carried away, suggesting a circus scene in the bedroom, complete with roll-up bigtop tent canvas. We gently disabused her of that one idea and cajoled her into agreeing instead to paint a sattvic evening scene on the soffit, with smiling planets and stars in a night sky above the bed {not to mention the drawings for this book}.

About that bed. It was built into the side of the bedroom and in an odd shape: too narrow and too long for any conventional mattress. We found the foam slab that came with the purchase to be only slightly less disgusting than the sofa and the shag rug and ordered a custom mattress. Finding sheets was a trip, but making the bed was something else again.

As a yoga teacher, mind you as a younger man, I was able to insinuate myself against the wall and under the slanted ceiling as we pulled the mattress out. By dint of nearly back-breaking effort, aided with both prayers and incantations, we somehow managed to change the sheets, admittedly as seldom as possible.

In the fullness of time, I had taken a page from our repurposed bathtub and remade myself as a yoga teacher. One of the advantages of our Fremont apartment was proximity to the five bus routes that went downtown to my one gig, at the Washington Athletic Club, and the two routes that went to my other job, at LA Fitness. As a consequence, more often than not, we slept in the apartment. Especially on cold nights, because we noticed that the wind had an annoying way of whistling through the walls of the floating home.

Oftentimes, when we did end up on the houseboat overnight in winter—even with baseboard heaters cranked up to the max—we slept in sweaters, long johns, night caps, and woolen socks. Additionally, we put ZsaZsa, our Frenchie, under the covers with us. A dog's normal body temperature is 102°, which is worth remembering for anyone considering the purchase of an older floating home.

On one memorable night, I got out of the only side of the bed that afforded an exit (Mary volunteered for the side against the wall, described to all her friends as "the pneumonia hole," which invariably caused them to level an unmistakable stink eye in my general direction), only to find the ambient indoor temperature a bone-chilling 51°, not counting the wind chill factor.

The log poachers walked by the next morning as I was doing jumping jacks, hoping to restart my circulation. "How are you coping during this cold snap?"

I tried to say "Terribly," but my teeth were chattering so much that I think they must have thought I said "Tolerably."

"That's good," one of them said, as they smiled and strolled on.

Two months and two portable space heaters later, thawed out enough to attempt meaningful conversation, I asked them if they had any idea why our place was so cold.

"Oh, it has no insulation, other than newspapers."

"Well, that's a fine how-de-do. Louise never told us that."

"When we lived in your place, just long enough to enclose the back porch, we pulled old newspapers out of the wall, some of them still legible and dated 1913."

That day, I went out and bought a mattress heater, which probably saved our lives and our marriage.

Once freed of the sofa and properly fortified against the cruel winter's chill, the place kind of grew on us. As long as one of us remembered not to flush or turn on the dish washer, the washing machine, or any of the faucets, while the other was trying to negotiate the miniature shower. As long as we avoided having more than one person on the stairs at any one time.

That we had learned the hard way, by allowing thirty or more people, half of them utter strangers, to watch the Lake Union Fourth of July fireworks from our rooftop deck. I spent the whole time futilely trying my darndest to distribute the weight evenly, only to find a seven-inch slope in the floor the next morning. This led to the first of many transiently effective levelings and marked the last time we were so generous with celebratory invitations.

We decided to take the plunge, so to speak, on a major remodel and then vacate the Fremont apartment, downsize, and move into the floating home full time. We thought we were ready.

The first-floor walls were bumped out in four places.

This would afford us: more counter and eating space in the kitchen; a bigger bedroom, with centrally located bed; an enlarged bathroom, with full-sized tiled shower and linen closet; a walk-in closet, ideal for skinny non-claustrophobics; even a laundry room. Our builder was so proud of the laundry room, he actually proposed a glass door for it, so that the aesthetic beauty of the new space would not be lost, even to the most casual of visitors.

Before any of this could be done, we had to make a serious effort to stabilize the float, which meant properly attaching the bonus log, hitherto attached with little more than 1x4s and wood screws. It also meant removing 900 pounds of water-logged Styrofoam and adding seventeen air barrels.

I helped our builder take the Styrofoam to the new dump in Fremont—a monument to dystopia (complete with viewing room!), the living embodiment of the Waste Land, a godforsaken place which I hope never to experience again—most likely the final stop for the sofa pieces on their way to oblivion.

Among the next items on the list were: a new roof with railing; new decks, on three levels; new hardwood flooring in place of the nasty shag carpet; new windows; skylights; new appliances; new plumbing; electrical upgrading; and a heating, ventilation, and air conditioning system.

Real insulation throughout was a must! We splurged on a heated towel rack and bathroom floor. Although most of the jungle scene had to go, we salvaged the painted door, on which still could be seen the river, some of the forest, and nearly one half of the leopard. Our artist friend returned to create a portrait of our beloved, departed dogs on the stairwell wall. She took one look at the sorry remains of the game preserve with the hacked-up big cat and repainted the door white.

Our contractor did almost all of this remodel by himself. In his spare time, Ben also was perfecting a fine sangiovese through much experimentation (and fermentation), which may explain why the job took nearly three years. This gave us plenty of time to delve into the mechanics of adopting him, in hopes of getting a "Friends and Family" rate for his labor. Also, to downsize a household full of stuff.

Furniture up for grabs for the family, the family of choice, the indigent, ultimately to anyone who would take anything, and the rest to one of two jumbo storage units. My entire Theodore Roosevelt collection of 300+ books, including several first editions, to Dickinson University in North Dakota. An additional twenty-seven boxes of books to the Seattle Library.

This required some stealthy planning, as no branch would accept more than two boxes of books from any one person. Once one of us got shut out, the other would wait a week or so before carting a couple of boxes in. We spread our largesse around four different libraries. We even recruited several friends to assist.

And here we are today, easily getting in and out on

either side of the centrally- located bed. We just have to make sure that we never get out on the same side, in order to avoid tilting the place. Either that or take the plunge and remove the rest of the Styrofoam, replacing it with an armada of air barrels. In any case, we are able to use both the dish washer and the clothes washer, while simultaneously enjoying a roomy, hot shower. And we have a clean sectional sofa. We are cozy, not cramped.

One of the select few members of our community who never had the pleasure of living in our home walked by one day, after all this remodeling was done, when we were once again on tilt, and asked, "Wouldn't it have been simpler to tear the place down, bring in concrete float blocks, and build a brand-new home?"

All I know is, we are trying to do our level best.

Getting Lucky

You never know what you might hear from an Orkin pest control guy, especially if you don't try to make conversation with him. You could simply let him into your house to have at the yellow jackets while you read the morning paper, or, more likely, cultivate your burgeoning social network over a cup of coffee. He might do his thing and be gone, and where would that leave you?

Oh sure, with fewer pests around the place. But think: what might you have missed? Everyone has a story.

Take, for instance, this specific Orkin pest control guy. Who just happened to be a lot more than what I had bargained for, when I dialed up the company and called for help.

It all started with his accent. I can detect a New Yorker within four words. Give me ten or so, and I usually can narrow it down to the specific borough.

This guy was definitely not from New York. There was no doubt about it; he was from Jersey. Northern New Jersey, to be exact.

"So, what brought you out here?"

"I dunno. I guess I was ready for a change of pace."

"Oh yeah? What were you doing back in Jersey?"

"Hey! How d'ya know I'm from New Jersey?" So, I told him about my gift with dialects, and that I was from New York.

"I was wonderin'. What part?"

When I told him Manhattan, he said, "But you ain't got much of a New York accent."

I explained that Manhattanites tend to have a less distinct New York accent. In fact, I don't think I have any accent at all, although some might disagree. I also don't think I snore.

"Anyway, I was a cop."

"From a Jersey cop to an Orkin pest control guy in Seattle?"

"Yeah, well, that's the way it goes."

This got me thinking about Eddie Feeley, who was a fixture with the NYPD and my favorite of all of my parents' friends. They invited him to the house frequently, because, invariably, he was the life of the party. He would grab a beer and head right to the piano and start pounding out a series of hilarious, usually off-color songs.

Pretty soon everybody would be singing along, even if they didn't know the tune. Then his wife Madeline would start dancing. Usually by herself. Maybe someone else would displace Eddie at the piano, and Eddie would tap the beat with a spoon. Or maybe he would regale us with the story of some famous crime bust.

Orkin Man interrupted my reverie. "You wanna know somethin' inneresting? You wanna know who was my great uncle?"

This wasn't really anything I was wondering about, but I took the bait.

"Lucky Luciano. Ever hear of him?"

Did I ever hear of him? Of course, I did. Everyone my age who faithfully watched *The Untouchables* knows who Lucky Luciano was: The Mafia don; the *capo di tutti capi*; the racketeer who was sentenced to serve thirty to fifty years in The Big House for compulsory prostitution and extortion; yet, who was released after seven years, allegedly because he cooperated with naval intelligence to clean up corruption in the New York harbor; and who consequently was deported to Sicily. {Okay, so I looked up these details. So, shoot me.} The gangster who continued to run the NY mob from Italy.

"Wait a minute. Didn't you just tell me that you were a cop in Jersey?"

"Yeah. I was."

"Did the police know you were related to Luciano?"

"Sure. I had nuthin' to hide."

"And they still hired you?"

"Of course. They figured I could be useful. See, I knew where they could find a lot of the bodies."

"So, when they found the bodies, you were no longer so useful, and that's why you moved on?"

"Somethin' like that."

This was getting really interesting. My coffee was getting cold, but I didn't care. I already had some inside dope on Lucky Luciano, from none other than Eddie Feeley, and here was the guy who could confirm the story.

Eddie wasn't just any old, extroverted policeman. Eddie was Deputy Chief Inspector for the Borough of Manhattan—the head detective. He had worked his way up from a flatfoot, pounding a beat on the mean streets, to the head job. Along the way he saw and/or heard just about everything, including the way that Lucky Luciano ran his "family" in absentia.

"We had a family friend, a detective chief, who told us that Luciano delivered his instructions via a 'mouth man'." The way this worked was that his designee, a man (obviously, in this patriarchal society) with a clean record and renown, would visit him in Italy, receive instructions and transmit them to the underbosses in New York. Whatever the "mouth man" said was taken without question as The Word from Luciano himself.

"Deputy Chief Inspector Feeley told me that the 'mouth man' was none other than Frank Sinatra! That right?"

"Of course, he was—one hundred percent."

It may interest you to know that, following compulsory retirement from the NYPD, Eddie moved to Florida and applied for a security position at Hialeah Racetrack. Management saw his résumé and balked at hiring him.

"Chief, you are too good for this job. Why do you want it?"

He told them that he was bored. They gave him a job, but he resigned after three days. The inefficiency was more than he could take. He then enrolled in the local community college and took a math class. At the age of seventy-two.

The Orkin guy also looked to be up there in age, so I made the connection. "Did your Jersey police force have a compulsory retirement age?"

"Yeah, but, as I told you, I took early retirement so I could come out here for a change of pace. See, now the perps I go after are a lot smaller. Step aside, while I blast these little SOBs." And, puff, a huge cloud of whatever.

The smoke clears, and he calls after me, "You wanna hear somethin' else?" I am back, rapt.

"So, one day my great aunt, you know Lucky's sister, calls me up and says to me, she says, 'Tony, I'm gonna take you out for a fancy lunch.' So, I says, 'Okay. Why not?' And we go to this swanky place, with red velvet walls and all, and they bring out everything: lobster *fra diavolo, suppa di vongole*, steaks, *vitello Bolognese*. Now I know that my great aunt she lives pretty simple. So, I says to her, 'How we gonna pay for all of this food?' as I stuff my mouth with profiteroles and cannoli.

"Next thing I know, the *padrone* is sittin' at the table, talkin' away wit' my great aunt, and I can only pick up a little bit of what they are sayin', 'cuz I never learned much Italian. So, he gets up, and pretty soon she says to me,

'Don'worryaboutit. There ain't gonna be no check.' And, sure enough, there never was no check."

Clearly, there are some advantages to being Italian.

Eddie Feeley, who was as Irish as Paddy's pig, had just gotten his math test back, the day I stopped over to visit him on my way to Disney World. Now, Eddie had pejorative names for every ethnic group you ever heard of, and then some. And his math teacher was of Italian extraction. Furthermore, she had given him a seventy, whereas he calculated that his test should have been graded a seventy-eight.

I grew up in New York. I had heard lots of disparaging name-calling. But Eddie was on a roll and came up with some real doozies.

"Maybe if I am a dago, she gives me a ninety!" It went downhill from there.

The Orkin guy pulled me out of the gutter, as he continued: "Before we leave, my stomach about to bust open, the daughter comes out and pulls me aside to tell me that her grandpa had a little problem and needed help gettin' some guys off his back. He went to Lucky Luciano. 'He made things right for my grandpa, and we never got the chance to repay the favor. Until now. You and your great aunt are welcome to come back any time. Anything you want. On the house.' And she gives me a big hug, like we're long-lost cousins or somethin'."

"With free eats like that, I wonder why you ever left the East coast."

"You wanna know somethin'? I am havin' so much trouble finding decent veal any place around here, I just might move back to Jersey."

"Did you actually ever meet your great uncle?"

"Yeah once, when I am around eight, we stop over in Naples on our way back from a trip to Sicily, and he invites us over for lunch. I got a photo of me and him somewheres."

"Really? Could you email me a copy? I would love to see it."

"Sure thing."

I am still waiting. Maybe when the swallows come back to Capistrano... or when the yellow jackets come back.

Orkin's warranty only covers one year.

Topsy-turvy

I am at our "graduation" from six months of yoga teacher training, newly retired from the practice of surgery. Surrounded by twenty-eight young women. There are two older women in the group, and they, too, are part of what appears to be a conspiracy in the making.

Oh, yes; I had seen them earlier that day, whispering over in the corner, out of earshot, casting sidelong glances in my direction. I knew something was up. Our teacher must have had some inkling, the way she was looking at me.

Actually, she always had an odd expression on her face when she looked my way. Perhaps it was that I was the only male she had taught in several years. Or, could it have been that I was the oldest person she had ever had in her class? I asked her about that once. It was near the beginning of our intensive six-month training. I was holding a headstand as she walked by. She gave me an inscrutable, upside-down look.

"Why are you asking?"

"Oh, I don't know. Maybe because I am old enough to be your father. I even could be the grandfather of a few of these gals." By this time, I realized that my being there afforded her a sort of personal challenge—along the lines of, "If this old guy can make it, I can teach anyone"—so, I could get away with questions and comments like that.

I might add that it's not all that easy to talk when you are standing on your head, unless you are Father William {undoubtedly, a yoga wannabe—see below}.

There was some justification for my comments, since I once had seen a photograph in *The International Herald Tribune* of a twenty-seven-year-old German who claimed to be the world's youngest grandpa. And there I was, learning to teach yoga at more than twice his age!

Mind you, I was quite comfortable being the only male in a large group of women, having four daughters. Even during that one year, that *annus horribilis*, when all four of them were teenagers.

I was even comfortable years later, when invited to teach yoga at a symposium for 140 young female physicians. The gig was so much fun that I did it four years running, even though it coincided with my birthday, which irked my daughters no end and made my male friends jealous. They were mollified somewhat to know that my wife was with me.

I now take you back to the training facility, on that fateful day. My comfort level is not as high as my suspicion level. And here comes trouble.

"We should go celebrate our graduation tonight, don't you think, Jim?" This from the spokesperson for the rest of the group. The most charmingly irresistible person you would ever hope to meet.

Taking the bait, I smile and agree. "Where are you ladies planning to meet?" Thinking, *Hopefully, at some bar, after dinner.*

"Oh, we thought we could go someplace in our yoga clothes."

"Sounds okay. Where?"

"What about your place?" There it is; I knew there was some game afoot!

Yet, I fell into the trap anyway.

"We thought it would be great to celebrate on a floating home."

How am I going to tell my wife, is what I am thinking. "Oh, okay," is what I hear myself saying. Now I have to make that dreaded phone call.

"Honey, you wouldn't mind if a few of the gals from my class stop over to celebrate the end of our training, would you?"

"Do we have a choice?"

Before I go on, let me say that my wife is off-the-charts "J" (judging) on the Myers-Briggs scale. In fact, a friend who uses the tool extensively in his psychology practice mentioned that he had never seen a client so far deviated from the mean. She is the absolute, undeniable Queen of Preparedness.

When we bought a new car, she refused to drive it for three weeks, until she felt she was ready. When she was invited teach Zumba at LA Fitness, she got herself certified at the highest level. Even so, she continued to take classes from a variety of teachers for another year, before she actually was willing to teach a single class.

Mary is one of the world's authorities on etiquette. She was mentored by, and soon became a colleague and dear friend of Letitia Baldrige, the Doyenne of Manners herself. Letitia once asked Mary if she ever, even once in her life, faked anything. Mary could not even understand how anyone could ask such a question.

"Good grief. NO."

Why then, you may well ask, would such a person marry, let alone even associate with, the likes of me, profoundly a "P" (perceiving)? To her, I am nightmarishly disorganized and spontaneous. My college roommate, obviously also a "J," uncharitably, but I fear accurately, wrote in our fiftieth reunion book that living with me was "chaotic."

"Well, we had some fun, didn't we?" I had to ask. He did not deign to respond, but I believe that deep down he was grateful for the liberating experience.

There was the time I came home from a long day in the operating room to a phone call from a friend, who happened to be a judge (the ultimate "J") who was wondering why we were so tardy for her birthday party, which we had thought—and Mary had written in her meticulously inscribed calendar—was the following day.

This was about as dire a scenario for Mary as one could possibly conjure.

What did I do? I handed her the phone and asked her to work it out, thus creating a meltdown of epic proportions. In my defense, I knew much less about the Myers-Briggs test at that time.

As if that isn't enough of a recipe for marital discord, I am an unabashed extrovert, and Mary the opposite. Fortunately, we do have a few things in common. For one thing, we both were English majors. For another, we love dogs. We have good table manners. And, thank God, we are alike on the intuitive and sensitivity scales.

"How many are coming?"

"Oh, around 30, if they all show up" (knowing full well that they will).

"What time?" The words are monosyllabic, the questions terse, as Mary is going into shock.

"6:30 okay?" It is 5:45 as we speak.

"Are we to feed them?" The words sound like they are being sieved through clenched teeth.

"We can just give them whatever we have on hand. And open a few bottles of wine. Or something." I should have left that last part out—the "or something."

"Do you remember what happened on that first Fourth of July?" Mary is showing signs of reviving and fledgling feistiness. Not of a mind to give in readily.

"Are you talking about when the University of

Washington Family Practice residents stopped by? I was their mentor. What could I say?"

"You could have left it to just the residents. Did you have to invite their significant others and numerous extraneous stragglers."

"How could I say no? It was a special occasion, and we got by, didn't we?" The answer—as you may well remember—was, barely. We nearly tipped our home over, lost three floatation barrels, and lived a sort of tilted Fun House existence until the divers straightened us out again.

"Anyway this is different. We now know how critical it is to distribute the weight on the stairs and the roof."

Mary is not convinced, just numb. Give her credit; she puts up a bit of a fight before sinking into a state of obtundation. No longer able to speak, she merely mumbles what I take to be an assent.

So, over they come, all of them. Twenty-eight nubile, young—and two mature, yet equally fit—females. All up on the roof, evenly distributed, for all to see, on a fine summer's evening. And see they do. All of our neighbors.

No fewer than four of the men on our dock stop me over the next couple of days to ask me what my secret is. I tell them Irish Spring soap. "What a fine fresh scent"… i.e., if it could work for a fifty-nine-year-old man, it might work for them.

"You are old, Father William," the young man said,
"And your hair has become very white;
And yet you incessantly stand on your head—,
Do you think at your age, it is right?"

"In my youth," Father William replied to his son,
"I feared it would injure the brain;
But now that I'm perfectly sure I have none,
Why, I do it again and again."
~Lewis Carroll, from "Alice's Adventures in Wonderland"

III. Far and Wide

Wrong Way, Righted

Florence is for art lovers, history buffs, foodies, and tourists. It is a great place through which to wander. There are delights around every corner. There are also pickpockets and scam artists just about everywhere you go. We knew all this from prior experience in Italy, what we had read, and what we were told by others.

Which is why we set out for Fiesole, rather than Florence itself, for accommodations, following daughter Katie's destination wedding at the Tuscan seaside. Fiesole is a relatively sleepy hill town, an easy seven-mile bus ride from Florence. We have a pretty good idea how to get there, as we approach the metropolitan area in our rental car, relying on a map in those pre-GPS days.

Unfortunately, we make a wrong turn near the train station and find ourselves inside the walls of Florence during rush hour. Although posted signs make it clear that unlicensed cars are forbidden, we are stuck in a bottleneck and cannot find the way out to save our lives.

The next thing we know, we are right in the middle of the historic zone. As we drive on, now maneuvering through sidestreets, the rain starts, and daylight ends.

More than a bit later, we are inching our way around the Basilica di San Lorenzo, avoiding jaywalkers and cars turning without signaling, attempting to get back to the main arterial by the train station, when we hear an odd sound under the car.

{In heavily accented English, through the passenger side window}: "Wait! Stop! You roll-a over my money. You ruin-a my business. You wreck-a my life!"

{Me, to Mary}: "What the hell?" I certainly hadn't seen any container of money in the road. Mind you, I hadn't been looking for one either. Just persevering in the Sisyphean task of trying to get the hell out of Florence. "Did you see anything?"

{Mary}: "No, but I heard a kind of crunch. What are we supposed to do?"

Meanwhile a large man jumps in front of the car and stands there, glowering at me. I honk; he doesn't move. The woman is now yelling in Italian. Passersby are looking. A well-dressed woman leans toward our window saying, "Just keep going."

Good advice, except we cannot, without first running over the big lug, who is clearly not about to move. Our blood pressures are going up. Sympathetic discharge. Adrenalin busting out all over. Fight or flight reaction. In spades.

Another guy, as if to be helpful, sticks his head in the window, which by now we should have rolled up but hadn't in all the confusion, and says, "Listen: you get out of the car; you pick up-a the money; you give it back-a to the lady; you get back into the car; and-a you drive on."

Advice proffered, but not followed. By now, we

were on to the scam. On to it, yet scared out of our wits. Windows rolled up, car doors locked, we sit there and sweat. I am visualizing what might happen were Mary to follow that guy's advice: *Once out of the car, she could be held captive. I would run after her, and the car and our bags would be stolen. Or worse.* So, we stay put.

The woman is still yelling, the big guy is still insinuating himself against the front bumper, the second guy is now pounding on the window. Nightmare scenario unfolding during what was to be our dream vacation. This will take something akin to a *deus ex machina* to resolve. Where is that *deus*, in our moment of need?

And Poof! Just like that, our prayers are answered, as the woman, the big guy, and the other guy dissolve into the crowd. The *carabinieri* have come to the rescue.

Eventually, we manage to find our way back to the train station, and from there the road up to Fiesole, where we find our *pensione*.

We check in and tell the kindly proprietress what happened. She shakes her head and confirms that we had been caught up in a three-person scam. Next thing we know, the family is calling. The proprietress had notified our son in-law's family, well known to her. They had been expecting to hear from us hours earlier.

As stories go, when passed by word of mouth, exaggerations become the norm: we had been shot at; we had managed to survive a hand-to-hand knife fight, despite multiple wounds; Mary had been abducted and miraculously found by the *carabinieri*, tied up and gagged under the Ponte Vecchio…

Give us a break! We are fine, just a little shaken.

By the next day, blood pressures normalized, we are ready to contemplate Michelangelo's David at the Accademia, Our credit card is in a secret inside pocket. We slip a folded 20-Euro note into a sock. Because you never know.

We take-a the bus into the city, and-a we walk. Safer. Better for the waistline.

Travels with Ruthey

{I do not presume to call her Ruthey to her face; the diminutive form of the name is simply a tribute to John Steinbeck's *Travels With Charley in Search of America*.}

"Would you and Jim take me to some of the national parks out west?" This from our then ninety-three-year-old friend from Philly, in those pre-COVID days, when one could travel about freely. Looking back, even the long lines at airport security don't look so bad now.

You should understand that Ruth is not your average nonagenarian. Now pushing ninety-seven, she has her own personal trainer, a walking buddy, and holds down a job. Furthermore, she holds the family business together.

Ruth runs what is left of Jacques Ferber Furs from a desk her sons set up for her in what used to be her dining room. She utilizes her law degree and intimate knowledge of the business in working with clients and insurance adjusters to clean up the mess which followed the total destruction of their main store in downtown Philadelphia. The building was torched, along with the rest of the block, during the one of the early, "peaceful" Black Lives Matter protests that rapidly got out of hand. In addition to their inventory, the fur storage facility, containing hundreds of furs, was a total loss.

In happier times, Ruth would walk to work every

day, check on the books, make payroll, and dutifully deliver lunch to her two sons. Now that the sons have put everything—or, more properly, everything that is left—in her hands, and she no longer has the store to walk to, they take lunch to her. Seems fair.

I thought about this purported national park tour. Lots of walking, but Ruth could handle that. Utah versus Arizona? The deciding factor was the central location of La Posada in Winslow, AZ. That and the Eagles. Oh, and Route 66.

I am pretty good about setting up trip itineraries. At least I used to be. I fear my skills may be eroding, since we haven't strayed further than fifty miles from home in over a year.

My grand plan was to reserve two rooms at La Posada for a week and drive from there in different directions to see the sights. This meant that we wouldn't have to pack up and move to a different hotel each night. In theory, this plan had considerable appeal, especially to Mary, who likes to stay in one place whenever possible.

Taking it easy, as it were.

Ruth had enormous appeal for Andre, from the very first moment he saw her, shortly after coming to Philadelphia to work for his Uncle Jacques. Andre had been minding his own business, as it were, winning amateur body building contests in France, when the war broke out. At that time, he knew next to nothing about Philadelphia, and less about selling fur coats.

Neither Mary nor Ruth had ever been to Arizona. I had gone to spring training some years before and managed a quick trip to the Grand Canyon between games. I was delighted to have a chance to go again.

Andre always was on the go as a courier between the puppet government in Vichy and the underground in Paris—until he was apprehended by the Nazis. He was lucky in one sense, because he was deported as a political prisoner and not as a Jew, which qualified him for incarceration facilities marginally more humane than those of a dedicated death camp.

La Posada was designed by pioneering architect, Mary Colter, built for the Santa Fe Railroad on former campgrounds, and dedicated in 1930. After twenty-seven years of operation, the hotel closed and became an office building for the railroad. Thirty-eight years later, the hotel was restored to its former elegance.

Other than that, Winslow does not have much to recommend itself, unless you are looking for Route 66 paraphernalia, of which there is an almost unlimited supply, or wanting to pose for a photograph, searching for that particular corner where there is a plaque commemorating that well-known singing group.

There are a few bars, a couple of dingy restaurants, and one nice coffee shop, where you can get a passable breakfast. Thank heavens, the restaurant at La Posada is first-rate. This was a must, because Ruth loves to eat, although she manages to keep her figure, as we say. In fact, Ruth is beautiful. Smart in the extreme. She has a delicious sense of humor and a great belly laugh. All of this makes for an ideal traveling partner.

Andre knew he was barking up the right tree almost as soon as he met Ruth on the beach at Atlantic City. This was about eight months following his liberation from the Nazis. During those eight months, he rebuilt his body, gaining back the forty pounds he had lost through a succession of three concentration camps. He looked like a poor man's Arnold Schwarzenegger. And Ruth looked ideal to him. She must have seemed to him special delivery from the gods.

Ruth was dutifully delivered to the Philly Airport by one of her sons. We met her in Phoenix, installed her in the back seat with our little dog minette (who always insisted we not capitalize her name), and drove to Winslow. We had forgotten to mention that minette was coming along, but Ruth didn't mind. Neither did minette.

Mary hates to read maps. More accurately, she cannot and therefore will not read a map. On the other hand, Ruth loves maps. She quickly became a self-appointed, back-seat navigator. This was quite helpful, except for the times when she got a little argumentative about the best routes to take. A back and forth with me is one thing; with Siri and Google Maps is quite another. If I opted to go a different way, she would quietly sulk for a while.

Andre knew better than to argue with Ruth. He learned this soon after marrying her, three weeks after the day they first met on the beach. Which also was the day he proposed to her, so quickly that it made her head spin. That and his impressive post-concentration camp physique. There is a charming photograph of Andre hoisting Ruth overhead, which Ruth has proudly retained for some sixty-five years. Shades of Mickey Hargitay holding aloft a smiling Jayne Mansfield in a publicity photo for her scads of admirers.

Mary is not a big fan of group travel. You would never get her on a cruise ship, let alone a tour bus. She won't stay in someone else's house either, although she and I did share a suite once with my brother and his wife in Maui. We were relegated to sleeping on a pullout with an inescapable metal ridge halfway down. That clinched it—never again.

Traveling with Ruth, however, was fun for all. Mary got to ride shotgun the whole time. Ruth, with all the maps a person could ever need, was in the back, sneaking in a surreptitious sweet now and then to keep her blood sugar level copasetic. If she felt that her blood sugar level was creeping up, for instance after polishing off a big meal, she would pull out her insulin syringe and jab herself right through her pants. No alcohol swabs for this gal. minette spent hours sacked out on the floor next to her, occasionally rousing herself to demonstrate availability for a little snack.

Not quite so very much fun for yours truly. I was putting in seven to nine hours of driving every day, getting quite bleary-eyed in the process. No matter what they say about Arizona's beautiful highways, distances between main points of interest are rather vast. One trip took us to Sedona and Jerome. Another to the Grand Canyon. We took in Antelope Canyon on one particularly long day.

On an even longer day, we drove to the Petrified Forest, the Painted Desert, and on to the Zuni Pueblo in New Mexico. That one nearly finished me. Yet the next morning, I was ready to head off through Navajo Nation, hoping to make it to the Canyon de Chelly and back before dark.

Andre made it to Philly compliments of his uncle, soon took over the company and in due course integrated two of his three sons, along with their wives, into it. His fur business was successful, even to the point of opening three satellite stores in high-end suburban neighborhoods.

To take a side trip through Navajo Nation is to enter a different time zone, really a different world. Compared to the rest of the state, the landscape is more subdued—suffused with an atmosphere of prideful moroseness—sparsely dotted with ramshackle communities.

I had forgotten to fill up that morning and soon noticed that we were perilously low on gas. By this point I knew how many miles we were getting per gallon, and I estimated that we had enough gas to make it through another forty miles of desolation. I found a friendly-enough-looking Navajo standing around outside a lonesome roadside fruit stand. I asked him how far it was to the next service station.

"Thirty-eight miles." (Borderline cheerfully.)

"Are you sure?" (Anxiously.)

"Well, I oughta know, I'm Navajo, ain't I?" (Decidedly, less cheerfully.) No reason to argue the point. He went on, as if he relished stressing me out. "Sometimes they don't bother to open the place in the morning."

If we manage to make it that far, we will wait as long as necessary. (Mentally.)

"It looks like there is a town in the other direction that's closer than thirty-eight miles," Ruth volunteers from the back seat.

"Oh yeah? How do we know whether there is a gas station there?" From me, in the front, as politely as I can say it, considering the gravity of the situation.

Not a lengthy discussion, because I am in no mood for chitchat, even with Ruth, whom I love. Mary is silently praying. minette is obliviously asleep.

We made it, barely, or you might not be reading this now. And went on to the Canyon de Chelly, which was spectacular. Only not quite as spectacular as Sedona or Antelope Canyon. Or the Painted Desert. And let's face it—nothing beats the Grand Canyon, after all. Which is to say that we were suffering from a severe case of sensory overload. It was time to pack up and head home.

Andre's trip home was the proverbial long way around. For over two years following his arrest and deportation, his family had heard nothing. During those years, he was moved from one concentration camp to the next, ultimately to a mothballed ship in Bremen harbor, used years previously by Goebbels for a propaganda film. There, guarded by a few Nazis and fed nearly nothing, he lingered for days. The ship was bombed by the British, who saw the Nazi guards and did not realize that the cargo was concentration camp evacuees. Andre was lucky enough—and barely healthy enough—to swim to shore, where he was, at last, liberated.

I certainly felt no sense of liberation as we drove Ruth to the airport.

"Mary will walk you to the TSA line. We can get you a wheelchair."

"Whatever for?"

We said our goodbyes, tearfully. After all, Ruth was up there in age, and you never know.

"Where are we going next year?" This woman is a force of nature.

There was indeed a next year. I planned a considerably less-complicated itinerary that involved a whole lot less driving. Ruth spent several days in Seattle, and we showed her around. Then we drove up to Bellingham and enjoyed the beautiful sights in its environs and along the way.

The following year, we flew East to surprise Ruth for her ninety-fifth birthday. We share the same birthday, and I couldn't imagine a better way for me to celebrate, now that the gig with the 140 young female physicians was a thing of the past. This time it was her turn to cry.

"You shouldn't surprise an old lady like that!"

For obvious reasons, we haven't been able to travel with Ruth, or with anyone, or go anywhere since then.

The last time we saw Andre, he was bedridden and emaciated, nearly on his way to a better place. Which was so sad to see, considering the vigor and *panache* with which he always had approached life. Because he no longer was able to remember how to speak English, I did my best to communicate with him in French. I told him how proud we were to know him. I told him that he is one of my heroes, and he squeezed my hand.

We are looking forward to giving Ruth a big hug as soon as possible. There is nobody like her. She is another of my heroes. A couple of heroes, Ruth and Andre.

Optimistically, we are making plans for a post-COVID trip after Ruth turns ninety-seven. We will fly back to Philly, pick her up, and head out on another adventure. Whichever direction we go, we will be thrilled to be reunited with our favorite back-seat navigator, map in hand, insulin at the ready—our dog Louis, a worthy successor to (never a replacement for) minette, at her feet.

An excellent travel team.

Snafu

"Here is your boarding pass. You are all ready to go." Meaning Mary.

"But he cannot go with you." Meaning me. She hands my ticket back to me without a boarding pass.

What the fuck? We are at SeaTac Airport—to be specific, the British Airways check-in counter. It is 4:25 p.m., and I am now beside myself. Yet, I still have enough presence to speak.

"What do you mean, I can't go? You must be kidding. Ha-ha. Funny joke. Here, look again at my ticket. Same as hers, right? We are traveling together. We are married." (As if that makes any difference.) "Look here; it plainly says that our flight to Vienna is scheduled to depart at 7:12 p.m."

"Sorry, sir. She can go through security and board, but you cannot." My blood pressure is on its way to the stratosphere.

"There must be some mistake. Something wrong with my ticket?"

"Oh no, sir. The ticket is fine. It is your passport."

"I have given you a valid passport. Take another look."

"Yes, it is valid. But the expiration date…"

I cut her off. I am about to get really rude, but I recover a modicum of composure just in the nick of time. "That is not until September 27th."

"That, sir, is your problem. You will not be allowed into Austria."

"But today is the 6th of July!"

"Correct."

"And we will be flying home on July 20th."

"Your wife may be, sir, but you cannot go." *Are we in the Twilight Zone,* I am wondering? "Your passport must be valid for at least three months beyond the date of your return."

"Since when?"

"This has been in effect for some time now, sir." I am steaming under the collar of my brand-new Travelsmith shirt. I had registered our passport numbers and expiration dates online with British Airways more than a month in advance. I had received no red flag warning. I tell her so.

"Sorry, sir, that is not our responsibility."

"Well then, why was the expiration date required for registration?"

"Regulations, sir."

There is a line behind us. I ask to speak with the supervisor, who pulls us aside. "What can be done about this?"

"Well, sir, I suggest you apply for an expedited passport." I know about this. You pay an extra fee for a new passport that arrives in three weeks, therefore putting the proverbial kibosh on the whole trip. Even worse— all our hotel reservations are non-refundable because I stupidly had opted out of extra travelers' insurance to cover this and other types of man-made disasters (acts of God generally excluded). I now am all about wringing the hands, gnashing the teeth, and pulling out what little is left of the hair on my head.

"Actually, you can get an expedited passport in a matter of hours. Let me give you the address." This, like so much of what is happening, is news to me. But it offers a glimmer of hope.

The place is downtown. I look at my watch. "Can I zip right over, get this taken care of, and zip back in time for my flight?"

"My understanding is that they close at 5 p.m." Reality check. It is now 4:42.

"Suppose I go first thing in the morning and get this done? Are there any seats available on tomorrow's flight?" She confirms that there are. One begins to wonder, *Are things looking up?*

We pick up our bags and lug them out of the airport, incongruous as that may have seemed to the other passengers at the departure counter, hop a cab, and head for the Fairmont Hotel for the night. We are simply too ashamed to go home and explain our unexpected return to the housesitter.

"Honey, why didn't you just renew your passport last year when I renewed mine?" Not quite like saying I told you so, but close enough. I am too upset to answer, and that is probably just as well.

The Fairmont is arguably Seattle's finest hotel, and we are given a lovely room, which we are not of a mood to enjoy. I call the Intercontinental Hotel in Vienna to try to explain and ask that we not be charged for the first night, but that doesn't go over well.

"Sorry, sir, but the room is reserved for you."

I already know the answer, but I need to try again: "Yes, but we cannot get there until the following day. Is there nothing you can do for us?" I get a paraphrased response.

More important that I get a new passport. I call the agency and am given a 10:30 a.m. appointment.

We head over to the office building at 8 a.m., just to make sure that we know exactly where to go. Although the office doesn't open until 8:45, there already is a long line. The mood of this gathering is considerably less than lightsome. We surmise that all these folks have run afoul of the same dastardly passport glitch.

"Let's go get something to eat. You have a set appointment time."

"Hang on." I walk to the end of the line and ask a manifestly unhappy young man what time his appointment is for. He tells me 11.

"Honey, you go. Just bring me back a muffin or something. I think I'll just wait right here. You go check us out of the room and have the bellman store our bags, so we can collect them and make a mad dash for the airport."

The office opens, and we all file in. Everyone looks stressed, I think mainly because no one seriously believes that a new passport actually can be issued in a matter of a few hours. I get to the front of the line at 11:30, pretty worked up about this whole thing. Suppose the passport doesn't come through in time for us to make the flight?

The clerk shows no sign of empathy. She has no idea that this trip was planned months in advance as a celebration of my second thirty-fifth birthday, which happens only once in a lifetime. It's a big realization for me, kind of new old. But for her, it's same old, same old: collect the paperwork, the old passport, and the money.

I am amazed to hear that an ultra-expedited passport costs no more than the moderately-expedited, three-week version—about fifty dollars more than the garden variety renewal.

"Come back in two hours."

I don't trust anybody anymore and come back in one hour. Same place, same faces, only now the atmosphere is completely different—festive, almost like it's time to pop the cork off the bubbly. People are laughing and poking each other in the ribs, as if to say, "We pulled it off," or "Piece of cake."

Me, I just want to collect my little green book and get on with the trip. A day late, and a lot more than a dollar short, yet somewhat wiser, I open the envelope in amazement to see something that almost looks like a real passport.

"It's valid, right? You're sure?"

"Sir, if you want to speak with my supervisor, you will need to stand aside."

Actually, I think, *I'm just kidding. And, anyway, we have a plane to catch!*

Back we go to the airport, in plenty of time, no less. Same lady at the departure counter. She acts like she doesn't remember, but I cannot pass up a chance to gloat.

"You remember us. We are the couple you wouldn't let fly yesterday. Or rather, you would have let my wife go, but not me. And here we are, back in less than twenty-four hours, with a passport that is valid for three years. Not too shabby, eh?"

"Here are your boarding passes. You are all ready to go."

"That's it? Not a single congratulary bon mot? Not a smile of recognition? It was just yesterday that you told me my passport was not valid, even though the expiration date was over two months away. We were terrified that our vacation plans were completely ruined. You must remember."

"Sorry, sir, we are very busy. Next!"

In the Soup

BEAUTIFUL Soup, so rich and green,
Waiting in a hot tureen!
Who for such dainties would not stoop?
Soup of the evening, beautiful Soup!
Soup of the evening, beautiful Soup!

Beau- ootiful Soo-oop!
Beau- ootiful Soo-oop!
Soo- oop of the e- e- evening,
Beautiful, beautiful Soup.
         ~Lewis Carroll, from "Alice's Adventures in Wonderland"

I remember the day my father, in a moment of uncharacteristic moroseness, put a damper on my normally sunny disposition. We were at the Belmore Cafeteria, on Park Avenue South and 31st Street—the other side of the tracks, literally (i.e., Grand Central Station) from ritzier Park Avenue. A fairly seedy joint, if you ask me, and long gone the way of redevelopment.

A number of the other customers nodded to my Dad as we walked in.

"Do you know these guys, Dad?"

"A lot of them. They are mostly cabbies, and we talk about the Mets."

Dad made a general introduction: "This is my son. He's going to be a doctor someday." Not much reaction.

I knew that he often would stop there after making a house call for a quick cupful before heading home for dinner. "Best soup in the city," he would intone, as if he had personally sampled the offerings of all the other 10,000 restaurants and really knew what he was talking about. Which is why I decided to check it out myself. I like soup as much as, maybe more than, the average guy.

"Dad, this vegetable soup is pretty watery."

"Nah, it's good eatin', man."

A cabby turned towards us and said, "Listen to your father. I see him here, maybe three, four days a week. He never orders nothin' but soup. He should know. Try the clam chowder next time. They give you free oyster crackers with it."

Between slurps, Dad looks at me and says, out of the blue, "None of the men in the family have ever lived to age sixty-six." Which to him meant sixty-seven years of age, because he persisted in this annoying habit of adding a year to every birthday.

For instance, as I am blowing out the candles on my tenth birthday cake, he is saying, "Now, you are eleven years of age."

"Dad, no. I am ten."

What he meant to say, were he not so pigheaded, or had he been an English major, was "You are embarking upon your eleventh year of life." That I could have accepted. Anyway, Dad was sixty-eight when he came out with this fallacious statement. Not the one about the soup, nor the obfuscation about my age—the one about the end of the line for Weber males.

He was correct about his father, his two first cousins, and my maternal grandfather, who obviously doesn't count except to pad the stats, since he was not a Weber. And perfectly happy not to be.

"Dad, what are you talking about? Look at you. You are sixty-nine years of age (playing his game, if that's what it was), and you are just fine."

"No, I'm not. I have a prostate condition." *Like virtually every other older male, you do*, I think. Like I have now.

Sure enough, my father lived to the ripe old age of eighty-two. My brother is eighty-one. And I am seventy-three, if you must know.

I remember thinking that I might be a throwback to earlier Weber males, as I lay in a hospital bed, recovering from my first heart attack, contemplating the fact that I was not quite forty-two. Fortunately, I have cleared the bar, and then some, thanks to modern medicine, skilled interventional cardiologists, Mary's obsessively healthy cuisine, and switching from surgery to yoga.

Be that as it may, I am now at a point in my life where former classmates are beginning to fall by the wayside with increasing frequency. My high school friend, Phil Peck, recently passed away from acute leukemia. A number of us attended his memorial gathering in Concord, Massachusetts.

The event coincided with the annual Theodore

Roosevelt Symposium in Dickinson, North Dakota. Although I had been there previously, I determined that this was a perfect time to go again, on my way back from the East coast. And while there, I thought, *Why not also take in some of the sights in South Dakota, Wyoming, and Montana?*

Mary was understandably a bit apprehensive about my setting out on this solo journey, but she doesn't read maps, and therefore really had no idea of the significant driving distances between proposed itinerary stops. Two years out from the trip through most of Arizona—being a person who really enjoys long drives and rarely has the opportunity to take them—I convinced her to let me go for it. As Theodore Roosevelt said, when asked why, in his late fifties, he agreed to travel 600 miles through uncharted Brazilian jungle, "It was my last chance to be a boy."

These days, the Dakotas are more or less civilized and fully mapped out. Besides, I had a smart phone to guide me and call for help if needed. So, off I went. I packed plenty of power bars and nuts, figuring that I might get hungry between meals.

First stop, Concord. If you happen to request Manhattan clam chowder, the server is quite aware of what you are hoping to eat. As opposed to their counterparts in the Pacific Northwest, who only know it as "red," as opposed to "white." While you can ask for Manhattan clam chowder in Concord as often as you like, good luck actually getting it. All they provide is New England clam chowder, the "white." Which I try not to eat, owing to the fact that I am hoping to outlive my father.

At the memorial, I told my former classmates about my travel plans, and several asked me to send photos from places along the way. They didn't say it, but I knew that what they wanted was to be sure that I actually made it all the way through.

The fact that I nearly didn't is only marginally relevant to what I am about here.

Second stop, Sioux Falls, notable only for the Falls— and the fact that it was rated the healthiest city in the United States by *Best Life* magazine. It is nearly as far away from the Black Hills as a person can be and still be in South Dakota. Yet it boasts the only airport in the state with non-stop flights from Boston.

So, I flew in there, picked up a little, lime-green KIA rental car, took a quick look at the Falls, and sent a photo off to those who seemed most sincere about my welfare. I found a restaurant that looked okay, but had nothing healthy on the menu, other than chicken noodle soup, which I ordered because they had never heard of Manhattan clam chowder (or "red" chowder, which would be politically incorrect in Sioux Falls).

"Do you want some crackers with your soup?" I nodded my head and was given two bags of stale oyster crackers, no charge.

I had booked economical motel reservations all along

the way, not looking for anything more than a simple night's sleep. Frankly, the place in Sioux Falls was the sketchiest of all of them. So much for *Best Life*. The smoke was so thick in my room that I had to request another room.

"All our rooms allow smoking, but we can give you an air freshener."

"How about if we just air the place out? I have asthma."

"Sorry. All of our windows are sealed. We have central air conditioning."

I used my inhaler liberally and was out of there ASAP, by the first light of dawn.

I-90 in South Dakota is one long stretch of east/west highway. It being late September, the early morning fog was considerable. The sun, behind me all the way, thickened the fog into a greenish-brown obscurity, not unlike lentil soup, flavored with giant neon chili flakes of intermittent blinding glare assaulting a lot more than my palate from the rearview mirror.

Occasionally, there would be just enough elevation to rise above the fog so that I actually could see the road ahead. For the most part, visibility was a major challenge for the first couple of the ten hours it took me to get to my next "accommodations," using the term rather loosely, in Spearfish, which is in the far northwestern corner of the state.

I did stop in the South Dakota Badlands for a few

hours, which was fascinating, but devoid of any food purveyors. And went on to and through the Black Hills. I can tell you that the area around Mt. Rushmore is like "Carney Town"—a nauseating array of garish tourist traps. A quick stop for photos of my hero (you know who) and the other Great White Fathers around him, and it's on to the Crazy Horse memorial.

You should understand that, as monumental as Mt. Rushmore is, Crazy Horse eclipses it by tons. Tons of the mountain, in fact the whole side of it, gradually is being dynamited away and sculpted to form this Mother of All Sculptures. Not even halfway completed after forty years. The work is so huge that the entirety of George Washington's granite head could fit in Crazy Horse's nose!

This gigantic carving, while originally requested by a Lakota Sioux chieftain, is controversial in the extreme, as the Black Hills are sacred to American natives. Yet the work goes on, tightly controlled by the family of the sculptor, Korczak Ziolkowski. Aside from a distant view of what is left of the mountain, there is a museum, a large studio, the family residence, and a decent restaurant.

The latter interested me most, after the long drive and nothing but power bars and nuts. Most of what they offered looked pretty unhealthy, but they did have one item that seemed fairly close to beef and barley soup, so I ordered their Tatanka Stew, made with bison meat. It was pretty "good eatin', man."

I should mention that an unusual affinity for soups comes to me from both sides of the family. My maternal grandfather loved borscht. I guess it reminded him of the old country. He would go to The Russian Tea Room, on 57th St., right next to Carnegie Hall, at least once a month and order borscht. According to my brother, who remembers such things, he invariably would go home afterwards and throw up. Did this contribute to his untimely demise, one well might ask?

Spearfish is a moribund town with a fairly dilapidated motel. But, hell, I was so tired of driving that any place with a clean bed would have sufficed. That the faucet head kept falling off did not bother me all that much. I was thrilled to find a vegetarian restaurant for a little dietary change of pace. The chef had packed it in for the night, but they were able to fix me up with some miso soup.

The following day, I managed to get lost in some remote cell phone-free and internet-averse hills for an anxiety-provoking hour or so. I was in search of Sturgis, which I found at long last and passed through almost without realizing I was there. Not a motorcycle to be seen; even the Motorcycle Museum and Hall of Fame were shuttered.

Next came Deadwood, home of Wild Bill Hickok— basically another tourist trap. All gaming tables and cowboy kitsch. I tried the fare at what looked like a decent restaurant, ordered a steak which looked good but tasted like shoe leather, and wished I had chosen the ham and split pea soup.

From there onward to Wyoming and the Devil's Tower, in homage to *Close Encounters of the Third Kind*. Tired of driving, I spent a good three hours circumventing the tower by foot, on the lookout for extraterrestrials, but finding little more than a few suspicious-looking humans. Disappointed, I returned to Spearfish and the same restaurant, just ahead of closing time, for their ramen with tofu.

The drive to North Dakota was challenging. High winds and heavy rain made for a full two seconds of zero visibility every time a big truck came from the opposite direction, splashing more water on the windshield than any wiper in creation could handle. The first time that happened, I was fairly sure I was going to die and nearly lost control both of car and bladder, but I got used to it. Just kept going straight, praying, and hoping for the best.

This went on for two excruciating hours until I neared my destination, Medora, where TR briefly had flirted with cattle ranching and cowboy life. I left the highway and opted for the old route into town, which would allow me a look at the foothills of the North Dakota Badlands.

Big mistake. The torrential rain turned the soft shoulders into quagmires. Sadly, I did not discover this until after I had pulled over to take a leak. The pulling-over part was fine, but the relief was transitory. Getting out of there appeared to be daunting at best.

Stuck in the mud, once again outside of cell phone range, with no signs of civilization in sight—this was worse than driving through lentil soup fog, being lost somewhere in the hills of South Dakota, or having huge semis pass me going the other way in a driving rain to beat all others. At least in those situations, I could keep going. In this case, I was unable to go anywhere at all.

No handy pieces of wood to put under the rear tires for traction. No cars coming by to help. Once again, I resorted to prayer, because I needed some help, which is pretty much the only time I pray—more often than you might think, which is a little scary for a surgeon to admit, even after retiring. Meanwhile, I kept trying the old back-and-forth, over-and-over routine.

After what seemed like hours but what was probably only ten minutes, I managed to pull loose and made it to Medora. The back half of the green KIA was completely mud-splatter brown, from top to bottom.

Medora has practically nothing to offer, except the following: two bars; a church; a bookstore specializing in Zane Gray; the Rough Riders Hotel, which was fully booked for the TR conference, and which features the only restaurant in town other than the Cowboy Cafe (breakfast only); a surprisingly decent motel, where I stayed; and the entrance to the South Part of the Theodore Roosevelt National Park, i.e., the North Dakota Badlands. Oh, also a gas station, but no car wash. For that I had to drive another twenty miles to Dickinson.

Embarrassed to pull into a city with a car looking like this, I made right for a car wash, drove through it three times, and then found a decent restaurant which featured a delicious mushroom soup that looked exactly like the back of the KIA prior to cleansing.

The conference was stimulating—even better, the mushroom soup, which was inviting enough for a repeat.

"Weren't you in here yesterday? Welcome back. Here's the menu."

"That's okay. I know what I will have."

For dinner, because the Rough Riders Hotel restaurant had no soup on the menu, I opted to give their bison osso buco a try. This made me mindful of my father, who, after ordering a bowl of minestrone at Paul and Jimmy's, our neighborhood Italian restaurant, always would inquire when the osso buco had been cooked. He only would order it if it was a day or two old, I guess to give the bacteria adequate time to impart their special flavor.

The first time he asked about this, the waiter assured him that it was cooked just that morning, as a result of which Dad told him to bring a bowl of Tuscan *pasta e fagioli* soup instead. The waiters at Paul and Jimmy's soon wised up to him.

"Certainly, *dottore*; the osso buco was prepared a few days ago. Just-a the way you wannit." We had no idea how accurate this was. Yet, the response satisfied Dad, who assured me, "That's good eatin', man." Good thing Dad had no daughters.

The Theodore Roosevelt National Park is actually divided, the two halves separated by seventy miles of national grasslands. Of course, I had to take in both halves, which made for a fairly long day of driving, hiking, and photographing. I barely made it towards the exit of the North Park before closing time. It was twilight, as I turned the corner to find a big bull grazing solo near the side of the road.

"What a photo op," I said to myself. Now I may be a tenderfoot, but I know something about being sensible in one's approach to giant mammals. So, I sidled up, real slow-like. So far, so good. The bison did not appear to care about what I was up to. He went on grazing, while I went on sidling.

As I rolled down the window at a glacial pace—about to snap a shot and skedaddle—he suddenly leveled the old stink-eye look on yours truly, as if to say, "SO, I hear something about you eating my cousin last night for dinner…" Snap, and I was out of there, faster than you could say Buffalo Bill Cody.

Next morning, I packed up my gear, moseyed over to the Cowboy Cafe for some pancakes, fresh off the griddle, and headed west to Big Sky country. Covering the last 300 miles, after driving for 1,500 or so over the preceding four days, started to wear me down. My adrenalin supply was dwindling fast. So were the power bars and nuts.

I allowed just enough time to take in Pompey's Pillar National Monument. This afforded a chance to stretch the old legs and climb some 250 steps to the top of the pillar for a nice view of the Yellowstone River. This could have been found on Google for far less trouble.

"Did you see that rattler by the steps?"—words from a young and foolish enthusiast just as I returned to the base of the pinnacle.

"Nope."

"Want to see it?" First reaction, *Hell, no.* Second reaction, *One last photo op?*

The only other time I had seen a rattlesnake was just after Mary ditched me in the hills of Ojai, CA. She saw it and heard it. I was a few steps behind, blissfully ignorant of the lurking menace. Suddenly she was gone (amygdala hijack), and the rattle was audible, close at hand…

I didn't stop for a photo then, but, having survived a close encounter of the bison kind, not to mention the other recent near-disasters, I was beginning to think, *I may be immortal.*

"Where is it?"

"Oh, it's all coiled up right by the stairs, a little way yonder." Yonder was back up about 180 steps. This was the macho thing to do, to act unafraid of a coiled rattlesnake that might, or might not, be asleep. So, I did it.

I had just enough time for a quick bite to eat in Billings, Montana, before heading to the airport.

"What do you have that's pretty quick?"

You guessed it—soup. Manhattan clam chowder, right there in Billings!

"Where do these clams come from?"

"I really don't know."

Truthfully, I really didn't care. Even when I was informed they had no oyster crackers. I just wanted to get home. This was a long, long journey.

"Honey, are you too tired to go to Jack and Koh's for dinner tomorrow?"

"Nah. I haven't had much opportunity for conversation lately."

So, we went to our friends for dinner. Jack served up his favorite old family recipe—borscht.

> *Beautiful Soup! Who cares for fish,*
> *Game, or any other dish?*
> *Who would not give all else for two*
> *Pennyworth only of Beautiful Soup?*
> *Pennyworth only of beautiful Soup?*
> *Beau- ootiful Soo-oop!*
> *Beau- ootiful Soo-oop!*
> ~Lewis Carroll, from "Alice's Adventures in Wonderland"

IV. Sound and Light

Enough, Already!

"This the Yale Glee Club?"

By chance I am answering phones this morning, although that isn't in my job description as president of the glee club.

"Sullivan Show calling. Ed would like your group to be on the show next month."

I think, *Maybe he's not kidding.*

"He wants you to back up Lee Marvin, singing 'I Was Born Under a Wand'rin' Star,' from the movie *Paint Your Wagon.*"

At my request, he sends us a simple and, frankly, boring piece of music, a far cry from the Mozart *Requiem* which we have been rehearsing. Although the Marvin gig is scheduled for the week before midterms, our guys are willing to do it, just for the chance to be on television.

I call back to say okay, whereupon the producer says, "Ed was wondering whether you have any football songs."

Now he's talking! Without hesitation, I offer to send him our Football Medley, hitherto sung, always with thunderous acclaim, to piano accompaniment.

Ray Block orchestrates it. An upgrade. Now we really are excited!

Saturday, October 11, 1969, at the Ed Sullivan Theater: We get a satisfactory take with the Football

Medley on our second try. We will lip-sync the piece in our tuxedos before a live audience Sunday (All music on TV in those days was prerecorded.)

The stagehands then assemble an ersatz Western ranch scene, with fences and a setting sun as a backdrop. An assistant producer tells us to put on our formal wear.

Whoa, we didn't take any along! I was told that we would not need to be in full regalia on Saturday.

Communication snafu.

By way of resolution, they ask us all to document our precise measurements: jacket, waist, and neck size; sleeve and inseam length; shoe size and width. Body by body, all different sizes, shapes, and lengths. Sixty-five tuxedos with all the necessary trimmings to be procured ASAP. Even shoes. Imagine.

Picture a truck arriving in less than an hour to deliver everything we need. Furthermore, the fits are perfect.

The Yale Glee Club, now in formal attire, is all ready, positioned behind the fences. Dude ranching, I suppose, is the desired effect.

Lee Marvin is nowhere to be seen, although he certainly can be heard by anybody within three blocks, because he is bellowing a veritable index of imprecations, a cascade of curses, an oration of oaths, an anthology of anathemas, a maelstrom of maledictions, a plethora of profanities...a whole lot of dirty words.

He lurches onto the set in formal wear, drink in hand, glaring around like a wounded bull in a *plaza de toros*.

Although his coiffure resembles an explosion in a mattress factory, this is quite apart from a bad hair day.

We are in three rows. Marvin staggers upstage and notices that a number of us are wearing a rather subtle protest button. It simply reads "ENOUGH" in white, against a blue background. He goes cheek to jowl with a freshman, saying, "What's this?"

Pinned against the scrim covering the back wall of the stage, the kid respectfully and courageously states, "Well, it's about the bombing of Cambodia. We think that's an illegal escalation of a war that we shouldn't have gotten into in the first place."

Whereupon Marvin, an ex-Marine, demoted from corporal to private—despite his Purple Heart—for troublemaking, yells, "YOU BEEN THERE?"

The young man, no longer enjoying his first experience on television, mumbles a furtive, "No."

"WELL, F___K YOU!" Then, for added emphasis, "AND F___K ME!" Perhaps there are one or two not listening; so, for their benefit, "AND F___K THE WHOLE F___KING LOT OF YOU."

A small posse of burly stagehands and security guards manages to hold Marvin down, while trembling make-up personnel clean him up a bit, trying to do something with that hair.

And away we go, filming. The *Paint Your Wagon* soundtrack rolls. We are being dubbed in, and the plan is for Marvin to mouth the words and wander through the phony ranch set, wending his way past fake fences from upstage to downstage center. A boom camera moves in, as he turns and heads off into the sunset.

At least that is what is supposed to happen.

It turns out that muddled Marvin mouths the words for the second verse while the soundtrack is playing his voice singing the first verse. He knows he screwed it up. As the boom camera focuses on him, he flips the bird, both hands.

"Cut."

Take Two is going a bit better. Marvin gets past the first verse, but he forgets to move his lips during the second. As the boom camera moves in, he ducks under it. I am impressed that he can do this without falling flat on his face, considering his manifest state of inebriation.

"Cut."

Ed Sullivan is called in. On a Saturday. This has not happened for years. He pulls Marvin aside, reads him the riot act, and boots him from the theater.

An assistant producer asks me, rather apologetically, whether we can return early Sunday morning—this time with our own tuxedos—to give the "wand'rin' star" another shot. Not the kind of shot Marvin would prefer, but anyway…

Sunday morning: We put on our duds and find our places. And there he is, offstage, dressed to the nines, looking a bit worse for wear. Again, with drink in hand, only this time it is emitting steam.

He walks more steadily upstage. Seeing no "ENOUGH" buttons, he keeps his mouth to himself and indicates to the director that he is ready to roll.

And, by God's grace, and Ed Sullivan's no uncertain terms, he pulls it off!

The first take is as good as it is going to get.

Sunday evening: Ed is back. The show goes on the air, in front of a live audience, really a packed house, complete with: plate spinners; comedians Jo Anne Worley and Woody Allen; Shirley Bassey; Topo Gigio, the annoying Italian mouse; a musical group called the Brothers Castro (no, not Fidel and Raoul); Lee Marvin, and the Yale Glee Club. A real variety show, a kind of high-brow vaudeville.

The comments from friends and family who watch the show run mostly like this: "You guys sounded great in that Football Medley. But that thing with Lee Marvin... was he drunk?"

My response: "You should have seen him the day before!"

About a month later: A thick envelope arrives at the glee club office. Eleven hand-written pages, in which Marvin goes on and on about how he really is a sensitive, kind man, too often unfairly typecast as a roaring drunk. I read this with a mixture of incredulity and disgust, recalling his foray of F-bombs.

I think, *Shame on him. How dare he pen such a pathetic apologia?*

But really, shame on me. Because I tear up that letter. In retrospect, I should have kept the thing. Imagine its value in today's market.

And here's the other thing. "I Was Born Under a Wand'rin' Star" actually reached the top of the charts in the U.K. and held that spot for three weeks, besting the Beatles' "Let It Be."

Which I could not do. I had to memorialize this event for posterity.

Cadge as Cadge Can

"Haben Sei noch eine extra Karte?"

This is one way to try to snag a ticket to a Wagner opera at his famous *Festspielhaus* in Bayreuth. Another way is to find a scalper, normally lurking around the periphery. A much surer way is to buy your ticket online, well in advance. If tickets are already "sold out," there are ticket agencies (Read: upscale scalpers) who always seem to have tickets, for the right price. Or, better yet, knowing the right person can get you right where you want to go—oftentimes for free.

Wagner aside, my wife and I have a particular affinity for *La bohème*. My dad used to say that Puccini's music would "get you right in the labonza." I always took him at his word, but had no idea what that word meant, or where it came from. Never occurred to me to ask him. I simply assumed it was somewhere between the heart and the genitals, and, taken in context, I kind of got the message.

He never said that of Wagner's music—only that to him it was "deadly." Around the house, he would play Mozart's *Eine kleine Nachtmusik*, Schumann's *Rhenish Symphony*, Beethoven's Seventh Symphony, and an inordinate amount of Tchaikovsky. He and my mother would attend almost any opera at the Met that hadn't been composed by Wagner.

So, of course, I studied Wagner in college.

Recently, I looked up labonza in *The Historical Dictionary of American Slang, Volume II*. The word can mean: *n. the buttocks*, which I am pretty sure was not what Dad had in mind. It can mean: *n. the belly, specifically the paunch*. Again, not Dad's intent. And then: *n. the pit of the stomach, as in: "That kind of singing can really get you right in the labonza."* Bingo!

Apparently, the term is boxing argot from the early twentieth century, where the point of punching a person in the labonza was to knock the wind out of them. Shades of Joe Palooka.

Where was I?

The more I studied Wagner, the more enthralled I became. I once got a standing-room ticket at the Met to *Tristan und Isolde*, whereupon—or, more accurately, where, upon my legs—I stood for a full five hours. Stock still, like a cigar store Indian. Afraid to move from my spot lest an interloper slide into my place. And I relished every moment. Good practice for long hours to come at the operating table.

I stood through *Die Meistersinger von Nürnberg*, another five-hour-plus marathon, as a medical student and noticed shortly thereafter that I was getting varicose veins.

Ever since then, I have preferred to sit. Not always in my assigned seat, mind you, especially during those impecunious student years. If I saw a primo seat from my perch in the upper reaches of the theater, I would try my luck at upgrading for the second and third acts.

I taught my daughters this trick, which three-quarters of them eschew as beneath their dignity. It has almost always worked at baseball games, especially during the seemingly endless losing years Seattle fans have had to endure.

I took myself to Europe between college and medical school, traveling hither and thither on a Eurail pass. Most of the time, trains were convenient and, some of the time, on schedule. Not so in Italy, where I made the last train out of Rome to Naples prior to a strike. Packed like sardines would be an apt simile. Not a seat to be had by the time I squeezed on board. After me came a young padre, hardly deigning to acknowledge the frail, elderly woman who gave him her seat.

The restroom toilet shortly became unusable, and desperate travelers took desperate measures with the sink, which created a most unpleasant odor in the adjacent environs, where I was wedged.

Almost worse, on the way back, I found the last seat in a third-class, three-person compartment next to a man who was busily devouring a salami sandwich prior to falling asleep, snoring, and persistently rolling his head upwind of me. I would move his head the other way, only to have it roll back again. And again.

Despite all obstacles, I managed to find my way, and rather cheaply at that, to Bavaria, specifically to Bayreuth. As I walked into town from the train station, looking for a place to stay (silly me—the rooms sell out months in advance), I lucked into a last-minute cancellation. The price was rather more than what I had budgeted for, and I still needed to purchase tickets for the opera (sillier me— the seats sell out a year in advance).

My knowledge of German emanates exclusively from what I have picked up reading about Wagner and attending his operas. Not that one can make out a single word of what a soprano sings, or more than 50% of what tenors spew out; *bassos*, however, usually can be understood. Supratitles give you a shot at learning the German-English equivalent, especially when the singer intones one word dramatically, e.g., *"tod,"* with a meaningful pause afterwards, so that you get plenty of time to associate that word with "death."

As opposed to deadly, because, you see, Dad was dead wrong. Wagner is not deadly. Long-winded perhaps. More repetitive than most, for sure. Voices hard to hear over the oversized orchestra playing fortissimo. Saving the really good stuff until you have been sitting there for over four hours. Okay. But not deadly. At least not to me.

So, here I was in Bayreuth, wistfully gazing at the *Festspielhaus*, 3,000 miles from home, two years since my Wagner course, with a hotel room, but no tickets. I asked a kindly-looking, English speaking *fraulein* how to optimize my chances.

"You must learn to say in German: *"Haben Sie noch eine extra Karte?"* Say it humbly, without appearing to know how to say anything else except *"danke schön."*

And there they were, the magic words.

I was blessed with a ticket for *Lohengrin* on the fifth try. The next night it took a bit more effort. By then, I was intoning that one sentence like I was born to it. After a couple gave me a seat for *Parsifal*, they said something else to me. It was in German, and all I could make out was "American" and "Elvis Presley." Having no idea whether the comment was pejorative or laudatory, I nodded my head sagely, said *danke schön*, and went into the hall.

The setup is a bit odd. In most opera houses, even if you cannot see much of the orchestra, you can see the glow from the pit and the upper half of the maestro. In the *Festspielhaus,* the orchestra is under the stage. Essentially, the slant of the auditorium continues past the edge of the proscenium to form the pit. Net result, one cannot see so much as a glow from below. When the audience is seated, the house lights are turned off completely. Not a sound to be heard—no sneezes, coughs, feet shuffling, programs falling off laps. A deathly silence.

Glorious music then envelops you from in front and

below, really from all around, since the entire structure is wooden scaffolding. The stage lights come on. You are made to feel almost as if you are witnessing a birth. Just like that, you are transported into Wagner's world of magic. And I was. I certainly was.

German music can hit you right in the labonza, but your reaction must be taken in due time with a large grain of psycho-philosophical salt. Wagner has his tender moments; he can bring tears to the eyes, as in the *"Liebestod"* from *Tristan*, or the farewell of father to daughter in *Die Walküre*.

Yet these moments evolve slowly, requiring patient endurance—in the former instance a full five hours. For the latter, one first has to sit through two and a half hours of *Das Rheingold*—to set the stage, so to speak—and then, the next evening, four and a half hours of *Walküre*, before the lachrymal ducts are jolted into action.

Puccini, on the other hand, pulls no punches; he goes for the gusto in the gut almost before you have settled in your seat. But then he is Italian, and therefore much more emotional than Wagner. Particularly in *La bohème*, where tears lubricate the eyes of the cognoscenti within the first fifteen minutes, from the moment Mimi makes her appearance on stage—even if she is noticeably overweight, which would be a bit distracting for a singer portraying a starving paper-flower artiste about to die from consumption.

Mary and I are so in tune with our respective labonzas that we can conjure up a tear or two at the very mention of

La bohème. A month or so before our daughter's wedding in Tuscany, we managed to squeeze in two viewings of the opera in Seattle, one live and the other cinematic. We planned a whirlwind tour of Italy around the wedding, beginning and ending in Venice, where the good news was there would be several performances of *La bohème* at *Teatro La Fenice* ("The Phoenix"), the legendary, burned-to-the-ground, totally-rebuilt, aptly-named opera house. The bad news was all performances were sold out, even via ticket agencies.

Not to be deterred, I mentioned this problem to my Italian soon-to-be son-in-law's father {hyphen city!}. He just happened to have a connection at *La Fenice*: the house doctor was a colleague. So, one phone call and, Presto! We had two house seats—center aisle, fourth row.

And there we were, handkerchiefs at the ready, sobbing our way through the show once again. No supratitles, voices a bit rough yet enthusiastic, the production replete with pure, unadulterated emotion.

Mary quit while she was ahead, on that high note, as it were. Because Mary has three problems with opera:

1. She has chronic neck pain from a fall on a wet gym floor years ago. Sitting for longer than three hours causes her undue discomfort.
2. The high notes attained by a soprano sound to her ears much like fingernails on a chalkboard.
3. I subjected her to two performances of *Lohengrin* within the first three days of her coming back into my life, at last, never for a minute imagining that she might agree with my dad on the Wagner score.

As a consequence, on all subsequent opera nights, she packs me a dinner, and sends me off, alone. This works for me. How can you be lonely when you are right there with Mozart, Verdi, Rossini, Handel, or whoever happens to be on tap that evening?

I saw my first opera at the age of nine. It was *Carmen*. My mother took me. I must have experienced it five times by now. There are several other chestnuts that I have enjoyed on numerous occasions. I keep track of all the different operas I have seen. The total stands at 137. Yet all pales when I reflect upon my lifetime of enjoyment of *Der Ring des Nibelungen*.

Call it a hobby. Call it a personal cultural rebellion against my father. Call it an obsession. Call it a rut. Whatever. I admit, here and now, to having attended twenty-three complete *Ring* cycles: nineteen in Seattle, three at the Met, and one in San Francisco.

When I tell anyone that I have attended twenty-three complete *Ring* cycles—anyone who understands that each cycle runs for seventeen hours over six days—they look at me with a mixture of incredulity and sympathy. I usually stop there and do not mention the other three I watched on television, or the five times I played it through on cassette, CD, and Spotify. And every time I go through it again, I feel I have found something fresh and new, which keeps me coming back for more.

Much like Tolkien's *The Lord of the Rings*, which, in fact, owes a great debt to Wagner, this is no simple fable of omniscient, powerful, supernatural beings, conniving dwarves, and frightening dragons—with some mortal heroes and villains added in, here and there, for good measure. We are witnessing the all-too-human story of the consequences of greed, overreaching, deception, and betrayal. Pretty much like American politics.

Just as in Shakespeare, much of what one sees or hears in *Der Ring* can be applied to one's own life.

Aristotle wrote about the catharsis that comes to the viewer of a well-written tragedy. The end of *Der Ring* is catharsis on steroids. The house burns down, the Rhine overflows, washing away all the malfeasances and dastardly deeds. A brilliant new day is dawning.

You are not far from that point yourself. It is, after all, well past midnight. No tears, just a sense of exhausted ecstasy. Your labonza cannot take another hit.

I write this with all due respect to my father, who never knew what he was missing.

Metamorphosis

"Dr. Weber, would you consider modeling in our charity Fall fashion event?"

I am nearly elbow deep in an immense abdomen, halfway through a gastric bypass. Mozart's gorgeous 39th Symphony is playing in the operating theater. Everyone, except the anesthetized patient, also hears the circulating nurse make this unusual and untimely request.

My concentration momentarily disrupted—with the strong possibility that my ears deceive me—I have to ask, "Cecilia, what are you talking about?" Asked, while trying to refocus upon hooking the tiny remnant of bypassed stomach to a considerably downstream piece of small intestine.

"We are planning a benefit Filipino fashion show, and we want you in it."

I put my surgical instruments down, look up, and ask, "Do I even remotely resemble a Filipino?"

"That doesn't matter. Magna is going to do it." Magna certainly is not a common name in the Philippines, which makes sense, since Magna is Norwegian. Also, six foot one, which is nearly a foot taller than the average Philippine female.

"Have Magna come in here for a minute." Magna also works in the OR and has about as much sense of humor as the average Norwegian, so I know that she wouldn't be kidding around, were she asked to verify what was said about her.

"Sure, I'll do it. Why not?"

"You are joking!" *Oops* (which is a thought you never want to cross the mind of your surgeon, even if it has nothing to do with the case at hand).

I finish the operation, make rounds, head home, and mention this invitation to Mary.

"Honey, since this is at least in part a non-Filipino Filipino fashion show, I bet they asked me because they really want you in it, too." Mary is gorgeous, herself a former model, but retired from that line of work for some years now.

"Honey (we do have other, more imaginative names for each other, but this will do for the purposes of this narrative), I won't be in it, but I will help you learn the strut."

"Well, I never said yes, but I never said no. It might be fun. And, hell, if Magna can do it…"

Word spread throughout the hospital that I, in fact, had said yes, despite my equivocation. I was getting attaboys from ward secretaries, the janitorial service, the kitchen personnel, and especially from a whole host of nurses. Because the hospital, like most hospitals throughout our nation, is staffed to a large extent with Filipino nurses. So many have emigrated to the U.S. straight out of nursing school that there must be a shortage of qualified nurses staying behind in Manila.

I have an affinity for Filipinos, truly the nicest people I know, almost all of whom go home at least once a year, and most of whom come back laden with gifts. Through the years I have been favored to receive vast numbers of *barongs*.

The typical *barong tagalog*, the national dress of the Philippines, is white, with ornate embroidered piping in front and hidden buttons. The collar is buttoned, the shirttails left out. The shirt is made of breathable, lightweight material, often pineapple fiber, and worn over a plain white T-shirt atop black pants, socks, and dress shoes.

I told my friends thank you, but no more white *barongs*, once I had about ten. They took the hint and instead brought me *barongs* in blue, pink, yellow, and combinations thereof. I often wore one to the office, especially on the six or seven hot days we have each year in Seattle.

Obviously, the idea was for me to model designer *barongs* in the fashion show. I was told that beachwear also was to be featured.

"Okay. I will do it, if you guarantee no on the swimsuits. I do not want anybody remarking on my varicose veins."

We rented *Zoolanders*, to see whether I might be able to pick up a few moves from Ben Stiller or Owen Wilson. I managed to mimic the pouty, insouciant look. Mary patiently worked with me on the moves. Mind you, Mary also is a dancer, while I have two left feet, like Eugene Levy in *Best in Show*.

We had our first session with fashion choreographer Raymond Villanueva, and it was an eye opener. There were thirty-two of us, ages four to seventy-four, and only one had any modeling background. Undaunted, Raymond appeared mentally to be sorting out those few who had some potential from the majority, myself included, who appeared to be nearly hopeless and, at best, perhaps could be melded unobtrusively into the background. Knowing full well that volunteerism is not to be discouraged—especially since every volunteer likely would invite at least four friends and family members to the event—he kept his sense of humor as long as he could and set out a daunting daily practice schedule.

He patiently outlined the plan and demonstrated the difference between "the runway walk" for females versus males. It was amazing to watch him walk one way as a male and come back the other way as a female. Impressive total gender fluidity.

We diligently practiced for a week, and the majority of us started to display some vague hint of getting it, at least of not totally embarrassing ourselves. Trunks full of designer clothing were distributed two days before the show. I was given three hand-made designer *barongs*, and, thankfully, no swimsuits to wear.

Experienced folks flew in from Detroit to help with lighting, sets, dressing, etc. Three of the tallest Filipinas in history, all professional models, materialized just in the nick of time. And last, but not least, the celebrated fashion designer, Toni Galang, himself.

Raymond scheduled a two-hour dress rehearsal for the morning of the show. This turned into well over six hours, in a desperate attempt to pull it all together. With a half-hour break before the event, we were told to come back in full make up to be dressed.

Mary, having had years of experience putting on her face for TV gigs, met me in the parking lot and fixed me up. The dressing area was readied backstage: 50% allocated to the three professionals; 50% for the other thirty-two of us, with no attempt to separate sexes. We put our first outfits on, while the audience of some 300 fun-loving Filipinos arrived and partook liberally of the generous hors d'oeuvres and drinks.

Raymond raised the microphone, the house lights dimmed, the stage lights came on, and the show began to moderate enthusiasm, as the crowd settled into their seats and digested food, alcohol, and introduction. We were cued offstage from both sides, and out we pranced for the opening set.

I generally enjoy playing to the crowd, whether it be: on the stage as a singer or actor in my callow youth; in front of potential weight-loss-surgery candidates as a surgeon; or in front of a yoga class—in person, as in the good old days, or by Zoom, in these pandemic times. I made sure that plenty of friends from both of my hospitals were there. Honestly, I believe that 10% of the audience showed up to support me.

So out I strutted, pretending to know what I was doing, and all of my audience plants did their thing—hooting, whistling, stamping their feet, and hollering. The rest of the models, backstage, were shocked at the commotion, quite likely more than a bit jealous, yet inspired to put a better face forward as their turns came up.

As one of the pro models was changing, she looked down to see a six-year-old boy, who unabashedly remarked, "You have beautiful breasts," before summarily being shooed away. During the next costume change, she had a private audience of four juvenile male admirers.

Although a few cues nearly were missed in the mad scramble for costume changes, and one woman who had joined a few of her friends in imbibing before the show stumbled out, shielding her now blurry eyes from the light, the show was pulled off with surprising professionalism. A DVD of the event confirms this. Also, the advisability of my sticking to my day job.

Quite a number of the *barongs*, dresses, and swimsuits were sold. Everyone went home well pleased, except for the producers, who found to their disappointment that the whole affair, when all was said and done and all the catering and facility bills were paid, had netted only $325 for the poor children back home! Better luck next time.

But count me out. Finished with surgery as well as modeling, I will stick to yoga...and writing.

Onward!

Act V, Scene One of Shakespeare's comedy, *Much Ado About Nothing,* is hardly underway, when the kindly, yet easily-duped Prince Don Pedro abruptly does a face plant. I sit there thinking, *If someone must get leveled, it should be Don Carlo* (his evil brother). Then it occurs to me, *This is a farcical way for the director to portray "Well, knock me over with a feather,"* as a series of revelations unfolds.

Ha-ha. Serves you right for being so gullible, I think to myself. But wait, Borachio steps out of his role to exclaim, "This is not part of the show!" The doctor in me gets the hint and arrives at the conclusion that, *It is time to forgo the "willing suspension of disbelief"*—i.e., this is a real emergency.

I am sitting more than halfway up in the capacious, indoor Angus Bowman theater in Ashland, OR. Although I have a clear path to the stage, another beats me to it and looks like she knows what she is doing. So, I stay in my seat, ready to spring into action at a moment's notice.

We are twenty minutes from the end, and all the hullaballoo belies the play's title. The Prince is ministered to and carted off, and an unplanned intermission is called for, clearly suggesting that the show will go on.

The Oregon Shakespeare Festival, founded in 1935, is a venerable and highly regarded repertory group. Their productions are elaborate and well-funded. In years past, performances were rarely canceled, even in the outdoor Elizabethan theater. That changed in 2019, when Southern Oregon began to be plagued annually in late summer with horrible forest fires and pervasive smoke. On top of that, COVID-19 put the kibosh on most of the 2020 and 2021 seasons.

Ill-fated is what seems to be the new normal for OSF.

Speaking of weather, having attended the festival at least 20 times, I learned early on to expect the worst in terms of cold and rain in early June. I always choose seats in the back two rows. I wear layers of clothing and take along hotel bedspreads and raingear, even though the back rows are covered. One does have to take oneself to and from the theater.

For example, one year, in early June, during a performance of *Henry IV, Part 1*, the heavens opened up with a vengeance. It was raining heavily until just before the show began, when the rain stopped for the duration of Scene One, which takes place at court. It began again to pour for the entirety of Scene Two, in the tavern. The rain stopped, as if on cue, for Scene Three, back at court. And, yes, it rained again during the following tavern scene. In between downpours, stagehands came out with the world's largest two-man wiper and swept the accumulated water off the stage, carefully missing most of the front-row patrons.

Anyway, to get back to the consternation at hand, the unplanned intermission was required because there was much to do—not only remove the fallen Don Pedro and patch him up, but also assess his mental status. Word was that he was okay, but understandably more than a little shaken, and not ready to go back out and finish the gig. Also, that his understudy was nowhere to be found.

Can't say I blamed him. With a mere twenty minutes to go, odds were approaching an asymptote that no unforeseen disasters would occur. This just goes to show you: you never know. This was really something.

The break went on for a good three quarters of an hour, while OSF personnel combed the outsized number of bars in Ashland, looking for the understudy. They may well never have found him, although they trotted out a warm body—could have been a stagehand or a janitor with acting aspirations, for all we knew—in street clothes, script in hand, to stand in for the stricken actor. He had quite a few lines to deliver, too.

I looked it up. You can find almost anything you want on the Web, especially if you know where to look. What you find may not be totally accurate, but who cares? There are no editors verifying facts, except perhaps when it comes to politics. Regardless, somebody who purportedly counted claims that Don Pedro has 183 lines in the play.

Whoever it was that OSF dredged up in desperation had to deliver the final sixty-four of them. If he could have lifted his nose out of the script, we might have had a better chance to hear what he was saying. Fortunately, little of it was of any particular import. The idea was to get on with it.

The stand-in's last line culminated in Benedict telling him: "Prince, thow'rt sad. (*I'll say; the beer's getting warm.*) Get thee a wife. Get thee a wife." Had the original Prince been able to put on a game face and finish the show, Benedict might have added something along the lines of: "And get thee a poultice, for, lo, thy head is well-nigh crack'd."

And so, to bed, well past midnight. With *Hamlet* on tap (*not to mention Budweiser*) and curtain to rise, myself in the audience, for a matinee the next day!

Not every theater organization can boast the luxury of an understudy for each role, which, at least theoretically, OSF supplies, sooner or later. The Bathhouse Theater, which played out of the old bathhouse bordering Seattle's Green Lake, was more of a low-budget concern and is long since defunct. In its heyday, the productions were reasonably good. Director Arne Zaslove was known for staging Shakespeare in unusual ways: *Othello* in Vietnam, *A Comedy of Errors* at Coney Island, *Macbeth* as a Kabuki kind of thing, and *Much Ado* (which obviously gets much play, everywhere) in Miami Beach.

My ex-wife and I were among the loyal few who religiously attended all their productions. The group would rent out spaces larger than their own 135-seat house for the bigger attractions. They were in the old ACT theater for *Twelfth Night,* a run which lasted until about then.

We were invited to the cast party on closing night, because we were donors. We walked backstage to find the room as cheerful as a wake for a serial murderer.

"Oh, Dr. Weber! So glad you are here!" *Was I to liven things up with my stand-up comic routine,* I wondered?

It turns out that one of the lead actors, a rather tall fellow, in his zeal to bound off the stage to the party, bounded just a bit too high in this unfamiliar venue, and lacerated his forehead on a concrete span over the side exit. Blood everywhere. Kind of put a crimp into the festivities.

"No problem," I assured his anxious friends, as I led him out the door by the arm, because he was a bit blinded by the hemorrhage. We drove over to my office, at 11 p.m., and I sewed up his forehead. We reemerged at the party thirty minutes later. It was like "Hail, the conquering hero." And the party went on.

Maybe he was concussed. Maybe he would not have been able to perform, had there been a thirteenth night for *Twelfth Night.* Maybe Bathhouse would have had Arne read his part, owing to the lack of an understudy. We will never know.

Seattle Opera maintained a two-cast system for years, which saved the day when the gold cast Siegfried severely sprained his ankle. Unable to dash around the stage— leading a captured bear by a leash, forging swords, slaying dragons, busting spears, taming fires, or flirting with Rhine maidens—he simply sat in a corner and sang. Meanwhile the silver cast Siegfried acted the part while lip syncing.

The opera narrowly averted at least two other potential cast catastrophes. The first came during a *Ring* cycle in 1984, when the Wotan barely made it through *Das Rheingold* before his voice gave out completely. Fortunately, the general manager was able to bring in a world-renowned backup, who arrived in Seattle less than three hours before the start of *Die Walküre*—just in time to dress for the role, with absolutely no time to rehearse. Amazingly, the opera was presented flawlessly. Everyone simply cued their actions off him.

Recently, the day before recording *Tosca* for a film version, the tenor had to be replaced. The backup got the call with twelve hours' notice—just enough time to rehearse the music with his vocal coach, catch the next flight to Seattle, and step into the role. A friend of a friend, I had this story from his own mouth over the leisurely dinner he so deserved.

Operating theaters also have fail-safe mechanisms to ensure that the show goes on, such as back-up generators, should the power fail. This requires the occasional test of the support system. On one unfortunate day, the lights went out and the generator did not kick in. I was in the midst of performing a gastric bypass on a 450-pound female.

"What do we do now?" I asked this question rhetorically, as everyone who was in a position to do something about this, i.e., not scrubbed in, was out of the room, groping around in search of flashlights. One was found, and we carried on, the anesthesiologist squeezing the oxygen bag, and myself peering deep inside a monumental belly and trying to identify the proper organs—for what seemed like hours. Actually, nine minutes by the clock until, behold, there was light.

Then there is the legendary story of the Portland heart surgeon, who, having become embroiled in a heated argument with the anesthesiologist, lost all semblance of composure and slugged the man. Rendered senseless, hence losing the argument by definition, the man was removed from the operating theater and his understudy finished the case, seething.

Yes, the work at hand simply must go on. Even when the surgeon (yours truly) has a heart attack during the operation. As luck would have it, the dissection was done, and the cancer removed. All that remained was to have the trusty assistant close the incision. Meanwhile the surgeon was carted off to the ICU. You know by the words on this page that it all turned out well enough.

The house lights dim, and the show begins, regardless of external exigencies, once the head usher gives the word. Some houses have closed circuit television for latecomers; some do not. Late seating in live theater is distinctly frowned upon.

Mary and I were in London and had tickets to Philip Glass's opera, *Akhnaten*. We allowed plenty of time for a leisurely walk from Mayfair, but promptly got lost in the crush of revelers on a Saturday night. Nobody could direct us to the Covent Garden opera house, and no bobby was in sight. Time being of the essence, I hailed a pedicab, whose operator pedaled furiously and delivered us to the door.

"That'll be ten bob, guv'nor." I only had five and no time to apologize. I tossed him the fiver, blessed him, and we ran for it.

"You are too late," but we were not of a mood to remonstrate. Up the stairs we raced, three flights. The doors were closed, but I found the other five bob after all, slipped it to the usher and in we went, as the applause died down, and the music started.

Indeed, the show goes on. No matter what. Nearly always.

Some Day Beethoven Will Turn 250

He died during a thunderstorm at the age of 56. How fitting for the genius who composed the *Pastoral Symphony*, which contains an accurate musical rendition of a storm. Not run-for-cover frightening, yet arresting. Who wrote a piano piece called *Rage Over a Lost Penny, Vented in a Caprice.* Who stormed out of soirées in a fit of pique on more than one occasion, when asked to perform against his better judgment.

Whose opening to the Ninth Symphony is a look directly into the eye of the hurricane. A look which is recapitulated in the fourth movement, when all attempts to soften the terrifying effect with tempting evocations from each of the preceding movements are repudiated, until the threat of descent into chaos is overwhelmed by a magnificent set of variations on a hymn of pure joy. A hymn which had been rattling around in his head for at least thirty-three years.

He could not hear the thunderous death knell, having coped with increasing auditory loss for over three decades. Nor could he hear the deafening applause that followed the premiere of his Ninth Symphony. His hearing was so far gone that he had to be turned to face the audience to see them clapping.

And I am sitting here on this special day, writing about my favorite pastime, listening to classical music. Today, Beethoven only, all day. Symphonies, sonatas, concerti, string quartets, overtures. Tomorrow, too. Because the fact is, nobody knows for sure the exact day of his birth. We know from parish records that he was baptized on December 17th, likely at one or two days of age.

I was a Music History minor in college, more or less. As much as a person who was pre-med and also an English major could be. I took two full-year classes in music history. The first concerned classical music in general. The second was confined to opera, with special emphasis on Richard Wagner.

In truth, classical music was the norm in our home. My father had a decent collection of LPs and a nice Fisher stereo system, housed in a beautiful wooden console, which sat in the dining room.

Dad had purchased the famous Toscanini Beethoven symphony set, the LP collection that came with a medallion of the maestro on the cover. I played the whole series, but the Seventh always seemed to speak to me in personal terms. The work has been popularly subtitled the "Apotheosis of Dance." Listen to it, and you will see how it got its nickname (from Wagner). I played it over and over, enthralled with the lilting rhythms, though not exactly inclined to jump up and dance.

Dancing is not one of my strengths. Oh, I had three years of dancing classes growing up, from sixth through eighth grades. I remember that the girls towered over me in sixth grade. Coming as I did from an all-boys' background, you can imagine how disheartening it was to see all those amazons sitting on one side of the room, with the lot of us shrimpy boys on the other, trying not to show how nervous we were. Wishing we could be anywhere else. Like trading baseball cards, pitching pennies, playing stoopball, or drinking cherry Cokes at Woolworth's after school.

But, no, we were cajoled and/or coerced into going to dancing classes instead. We hated it. Dancing with the instructor who led us was one thing, but dancing with some awkward, gigantic girl with white gloves and braces was quite another. There were only so many times a person could pull the "I don't feel so good today, Mom." Only so many trips to the bathroom. Sooner or later, one had to face the music.

Which gets me back to Beethoven. Because, for me, all musical journeys lead back to him anyway. I took piano lessons from an exceedingly patient teacher named Bill Korff on Mom's 1937 Steinway baby grand. This went on for about two years.

Bill obligingly would play for me the things that I had been assigned but never managed to practice during the preceding week. Truthfully, I did put some effort into

Beethoven's *Für Elise*—nearly got the first section down. I still enjoy listening to it.

I am not sure why the lessons stopped, although I remember being glad they did. Possibly, Bill came to the conclusion that I was a hopeless case. It could have been that Mom, who progressed much further than I with piano study, realized that she was wasting her money. I recall telling her that it would have to be either dancing classes or piano lessons, wishing it could be neither.

Years later, I regretted not taking my lessons seriously. The love of music was there, the piano was there, the teacher was available, but the student was not ready.

After some time, Mom's piano made its way across the country to my house in Edmonds, WA. It took a more than a few weeks for it to be rehabilitated, as it had sat unplayed for decades in a variety of damp basements. New felt, lots of lubrication for the pedal and key action, some deep cleaning, and tuning and retuning—once again, it was playable.

I encouraged the kids to take lessons. Emily, my oldest, was the most diligent, actually making it through two recitals. I managed to plunk out a duet or two with her along the way. Sadly, T-ball, ballet, and swim team relegated the piano to lost-cause status. Katie got one recital under her belt before saying "*No mas.*" She and I never tried any duets. Betsy took about 10 lessons and kept complaining that the teacher farted too much. Joey never sat at the piano, even for a photo.

Sort of like their baby books: Emily's is completed and fully documented; Katie's is maybe halfway there; Betsy's has nothing but photos, none of them mounted; Joey never got her own baby book.

Mom's piano still sits in Edmonds, neglected once again, save as a repository for family photos. I plan to donate it to the University of Washington or to Cornish University in Mom's memory. Along with the bench, the mahogany side chair and the nearly 85-year-old books of Bach, Mozart, Chopin, and Schumann piano pieces. And my copy of *Für Elise.*

Jonathan Biss obviously was not one to neglect his piano lessons. Perhaps his mastery of the Beethoven piano repertoire started with *Für Elise.* These days, his special niche are the thirty piano sonatas. A professor at Philadelphia's Curtis School of Music, he created *Exploring Beethoven's Piano Sonatas,* a free video course on several of the most famous of the lot. This course has reached more than 150,000 students in more than 185 countries.

Beginning in late 2019, in the lead-up to the 250th anniversary of Beethoven's birth, Biss dedicated an entire year to performing Beethoven's piano sonatas. Mary and I bought tickets for two evenings with Beethoven and Biss at the University of Washington's Meany Hall. We were disappointed to hear that the first was canceled due to an untimely indisposition.

Biss appeared fully recovered for the second concert, where he rattled off five complete sonatas—from memory! I had seen Vladimir Horowitz and Alfred Brendel pull off something similar. Horowitz had chosen Yale's Woolsey Hall during my sophomore year to be the scene of his reemergence from one of his lengthy artistic pauses. His artistry was legendary, and his memory I thought unparalleled, as he played Chopin for a full two hours, purely from recollection.

And Brendel did the same with Schubert, at Meany Hall. I remember someone coughing repeatedly as he played, causing this most intense of keyboard artists to wince with each cough. He stopped playing in the middle of a cascade of arpeggios, folded his arms, and leveled what music critic and friend Melinda Bargreen described as a "basilisk stare" in the general direction of the incessant cougher. Talk about turning a person to stone (a skill evidently not limited to basilisks); you never heard another peep from that quarter. Brendel picked up from where he left off, as if nothing had interrupted his concentration.

Jonathan Biss matched them both. He was so focused on what he was doing that he hardly showed any sign of awareness of the audience. It was almost like Beethoven at the debut of his Ninth Symphony, except the composer was intensely leafing through the score and stone deaf, whereas Bliss was deep into the score in his head.

An announcement was made that Biss had agreed to a "make up" performance the following evening of the program that he had cancelled previously. This was to be in a much smaller recital hall. Mary and I jumped at the chance to hear him again.

We arrived half an hour early, as it was festival seating. Apparently, so did everybody else. Disappointed that we would be relegated to far-side seats affording no view of fingers flying across the keyboard, we waited our turn to enter the venue.

I noticed a small throng surrounding a woman on the floor, blocking access to the aisle on the keyboard side. I also spotted two empty seats. Quick thinking was the order of the moment.

{In a loud, commanding voice}: "I am a doctor. Can I help?"

{*Sotto voce*, to Mary}: "Honey, scoot around the bunch of folks, run up the aisle and snag those seats."

And everyone made way—for both of us.

The woman, herself a retired piano teacher and lifelong Beethoven enthusiast, had slipped coming down the aisle and fractured her wrist. She was in shock from the pain. I ministered what aid and consolation I could muster and stayed with her until the EMTs came, splinted the wrist, and took her and her friend to the ER.

Whereupon, I joined Mary in what was to have been their seats. I was so excited that I left my hat on the floor.

A nurse who had been attending the injured party brought the hat up to me.

"Thank you, doctor. We were all so glad that you were there to help out."

"No, thank you. Really."

Jonathan Biss played four more sonatas. From memory. Nine over the course of two successive evenings. A phenomenal accomplishment of pianistic bravura, to my way of thinking. I wonder whether Horowitz or Brendel could have equaled it.

Although I was not cut out to be a pianist, I did go on to cut out quite a few organs. I also did quite a bit of singing in my day: church youth choir; grade and high school choirs; *a cappella* singing groups in high school and college; the Yale Glee Club, where I went on to be president; musicals and an annual Christmas choir in medical school.

Let's stop right there, so I can elaborate. I took the leading role in two musicals. This required some dancing. What I learned in dancing class, as far as it went, served me well enough. More importantly, the choreographer took pity on me.

The Christmas chorus was something I organized and directed. Thank God, I had a classmate who could play the piano and help me teach the parts.

The Dean asked me to provide the music for our graduation processional, which I was happy to do. I picked the pieces, transferred them to a cassette, and timed it all out, so that I could march out to a favorite dramatic selection from Handel's *Water Music*. I stood by the door with a stopwatch, exhorting my classmates to step lively or slow down as needed. Thus, my entry proceeded without a hitch.

But back to Beethoven. One my fondest memories is performing his Ninth Symphony at Carnegie Hall. This opportunity came about because Maestro Leopold Stokowski wanted to celebrate his ninetieth birthday by leading the Ninth at Carnegie. Although he was long retired from the Philadelphia Orchestra, the group was delighted to play once more under his baton. And he invited the Yale Glee Club to supply the chorus.

We were only sixty strong, whereas the Maestro called for a hundred voices. This proved to be a simple fix. We put the word out to Glee Club alums and easily came up with the requisite number. Although I had attended quite a few concerts at Carnegie Hall, I cannot overexaggerate the thrill of entering that famous venue for the first and only time as a performer. It was an unforgettable experience. A bit extreme in terms of vocal demands, yet well worth the effort.

My study of music history is ongoing. Never really stopped, other than an artistic pause of some nine years for medical school and surgical residency. Some people still read. More, it seems, listen to music. I do both. Often at the same time. Drives Mary nuts to wake up to the

Egmont Overture, but she indulges me on special days, like Beethoven's 250th birthday. Which, as I indicated, we are celebrating for two days, to be sure we get it right.

In fact, Beethoven never accepted that he was born in 1770, despite having been shown his baptismal records on three different occasions. He tried to convince everyone that he was born in 1772. This is the kind of thing my mother used to do, although she tried to shave anywhere from three to fifteen years off her age, depending upon her whim and the gullibility potential of the one whom she was trying to bamboozle at that particular moment.

Beethoven also harbored a not-so secret fantasy that he was the illegitimate son of royalty. In truth, his father was a sometime no-count musician and full-time wino. Fortunately, Ludwig inherited good musical genes from his grandfather. Sadly, he also got the taste for overindulgence in the fruit of the vine from his father.

As Beethoven was ending his days in the final ravages of cirrhosis, he agreed to receive extreme unction, even as a non-believer. Shortly thereafter during the thunder he could not hear, he lifted his right arm with clenched fist towards the heavens in a final gesture of defiance.

In 1806, two decades earlier, he had written the following note to his long-time friend and patron, Prince Karl Lichnowsky: "Prince, what you are, you are by an accident of birth; what I am, I am through my own efforts. There have been thousands of princes and will be thousands more. There is only one Beethoven."

Happy 250th birthday. If not today, then tomorrow. If not this year, then whenever.

V. Fauna and Flora

Hair of the Dog

The way the argument went, "If you are old enough to fight for your country, you are old enough to drink." The lawmakers in Connecticut, Massachusetts, Pennsylvania, and New Jersey didn't agree and left the minimum drinking age at twenty-one. New York set theirs at eighteen. You can imagine the traffic of eighteen- to twenty-year-olds across state lines.

The fact was that most New York City hotel bars could care less how old you were, so long as you could pay the bill. You didn't even need to show a fake ID in some places. Believe me when I say that we knew where those places were.

It was a relatively simple matter to cozy up to the bar at the Biltmore or the Roosevelt and order a Mai Tai or a Tom Collins. We generally went for the sweeter cocktails, because we really didn't like to drink all that much. We did it just to be able to boast that we got served. At sixteen, maybe even younger.

I put away three Screwdrivers in one underage evening. The first one tasted good, the second so-so, and the third was downed purely for the effect. That effect was etched so vividly in my mind that I have never felt the remotest urge for another Screwdriver since.

We were kids, after all. Of course, we were testing our

limits and didn't have any idea when enough was enough. One night, for instance, I came home from a party, threw my clothes in the toilet, and urinated in the hamper!

Consider what befell Billy, for example. We were at a friend's apartment. The parents seemed not to be around, but the liquor surely was. We filled the bathtub up (with water, not gin) and convinced Billy that the feds were on their way.

"What should I do? My parents will kill me if they find out I have been drinking." The words did not come out as clearly as they are in front of you now, but we expected a reaction like that, so we knew what he was trying to say.

"We think you should hide in here until they are gone."

"Okay, okay. I will do it…What, here in the bathroom?"

"They won't ever find you if you hide under the water."

And so, he did. Fully clothed. Shoes and all.

He soon popped up, and piped up, "Are they gone now?"

"Shh, not yet. Hide again."

He remained in the tub until we gave him the all-clear signal. His gratitude was sincere. "Whew. That was a close call!"

Half of the group repaired to my house for the rest of the night. Billy paid our carfare with the twenty-dollar bill his mother had advised that he keep in his sock, "Because you never know." The bill was sodden, to which the cabby took exception, but I told him to keep the change (about fourteen dollars) and sealed the deal. An easy fix, since it wasn't my money. Billy was still too far into the throes of alcohol-induced bonhomie to complain about over-tipping.

I woke up the following morning surprised and not at all amused to find a considerable amount of vomit on the pillowcase next to my head. Always resourceful, I stuffed the befouled bed linens into a clean pillowcase and headed to the laundry around the corner. I brought my friend Scotty along for moral support.

"What you got in there?"

"Oh, just a second pillowcase and a set of sheets."

The Chinese proprietor threw me a stink eye every bit as foul as the contents, while I shrugged my shoulders and nodded my head in Scotty's direction, as if to say "It ain't me, babe."

Half a century later, I reminded Scott of the story. "Of course, I remember the way you sandbagged me. Just wait and see what happens if you ever come to my house for a visit." One reason to be glad that nobody is visiting anybody during the pandemic. Not that I am expecting an invitation to his place, but, if it comes and travel is safe again, I had better think of some reason to decline.

Other than throwing up once or twice, I seemed always to have been able to hold my liquor. One exception came the evening my roommate, Bob, and I learned to play squash. We borrowed racquets and a ball and headed off to the court on a Saturday evening. We must have played fifteen games in a row before bagging it and moving on to a party. We went right to the punch bowl and drank glass after glass to quench our thirst.

"Whoa, you guys need to slow down with that stuff. It's methyl alcohol." Naïve as we were about methyl versus ethyl, we disregarded the admonition and kept drinking.

The next thing I remembered was sitting in a chair in our living room, watching Bob attempt to close the drapes. WHAAP, as the drapes got propelled from one side to the other. FWAAP, as he took a big swipe and sent them flying over to the other side. And back. And forth.

"Ha-ha," I said. "You are drunk."

He gave up and lurched to the lower bunk of our bedroom, where he stayed for the greater part of the next twenty-four hours, moaning intermittently. When daylight came streaming through the uncovered windows, I was in the same chair, with my pants down around my ankles.

In the bathroom, after sleeping it off for half a day, I met one of the guys from across the hall, who looked at me with a distinctly odd expression that any fool, even one more than a bit hung over and not seeing all that clearly, could discern.

"Glad you are okay."

"Barely. Why do you say that? And why are you looking at me like that?"

"Because you were sitting on the pot for over two hours late last night."

"I was? What, were you timing me?"

He was writing a term paper and noticed me sitting

in one of the stalls with the door open. He asked me if I was all right, and I answered politely and reflexively, I am told, inquiring about the state of his health. When he came back over an hour later to brush his teeth, there I was, no change in position or status of stall door. He again asked me if there was anything wrong, to which I responded, apparently coherently, in the negative.

Thinking my behavior distinctly aberrant, he mentioned the gross encounters of the turd kind to his roommate, who was burning the proverbial night oil in preparation for a mid-term exam. Apparently. I was still in the aforementioned stall an hour later, when the roommate performed his final ablutions. At some point after that, I must have made it back to our rooms and onto the chair, without ever pulling my pants back up. Or flushing.

It's amazing that I didn't trip somewhere along the way. Maybe I did.

I have just described what is known as a blackout. The story is funny and harmless enough. Yet consider the experience of a classmate, who drove back from the Yale-Penn football game, only to wake up stretched out in a booth in the West Haven Ho-Jo's (Howard Johnson's, for you young'uns), with absolutely no memory of how he got there (in his own car, which he somehow managed to drive).

After my escapade and hearing about this other, I vowed never again to drink in excess of moderation. My friend Billy has, to this day, not touched anything stronger than a glass or two of wine.

Which reminds me of the date from hell. Now is as good a time as ever to describe it. Call it a confession. I have tried not to think about it for the last half century.

I had met this girl at a school mixer. She gave me her phone number, and I followed up and asked her out. I arrived at her apartment, where I was greeted by her mother, in a bathrobe and slippers, disheveled and obviously inebriated. She attempted to articulate something or other by way of making conversation until the girl emerged.

I took her to Trude Heller's, a night club in Greenwich Village that I heard would serve alcohol to just about anybody. About two cocktails into the evening, I noticed a sign on the table next to ours that announced a cover charge. I knew how much I had on me, and I knew I couldn't cover the cover charge. No credit cards back then except American Express, which I did not have.

So, I sat there, sweat beginning to bead on the bean, trying to come up with a plan.

"Ready for another drink?" This from the waiter, for the third time. Not wishing to look cheap, I said okay.

I was starting to panic. In desperation, I asked my date, "How much do you have on you?"

"Maybe seventy-five cents." Back in those days, when a girl was asked out, she was neither expected nor allowed to pay. It was a different time. Before the microwave even.

I excused myself, found the phone booth {Look this up in Wikipedia.}, and called my brother. This seemed a more prudent plan than having to cope with the wrath of an irate parent.

"I am in a jam. Can you come over and help me out?"

"Sorry, Jimmy. It's past 1 a.m., and I am in bed. You will need to call Dad." And he hung up. Just like that.

This was getting worse and worse. What choice did I have?

Dad, not at all pleased, to say the least, barked, "Put the manager on." They talked.

"How much you got there, son?" I told him. I was way short. I promised to pay him the next day. I even offered him my wristwatch as collateral, which he declined. Dad had come through somehow.

Gratefully, I gave the man all I had.

Maybe the girl was thinking that this was quite the adventure. I was not enjoying one bit of it.

Oh, shit, I realized, *I don't have the money to get this girl home.*

With some quick thinking, I hailed a cab and gave the driver directions to our house. Mom slept on the second floor, Dad on the third—twin beds taken to the extreme. I had already awakened Dad and didn't dare try that again. I had the cabbie and the girl wait outside and tiptoed in.

We had a Yorkie who would come unglued anytime anyone touched one certain stairway step. Even if one skipped the dreaded step, hackles would go up, and the dog would go off. Which he did, on cue, as the whole house was awakened. Lights on everywhere. Audible imprecations abundantly evident.

I dashed into Mom's room, gave her an eight-or-ten-word explanation that made little or no sense, grabbed a few bills from her purse, tried to get the dog to clam up without success, and whipped back out to the cab like a bumbling thief in the night. Took the girl home and paid the fare, leaving me with nothing more than bus fare. At 2 a.m., and who knew whether buses ran at such an hour?

So, I started walking. And, of course, it started to rain. You guessed it; no raincoat. Remember rubbers? No, not that kind. The other kind! Well, I didn't have those either. The wind was howling, with nary a bus in sight. In point of fact, I did see one, but heading the wrong way. And me, nearly four miles from home. About as soaked as Bathtub Billy.

Wouldn't you know it? Maybe five blocks from home a bus going my way rumbled by. *Forget it,* I thought, or maybe I said it out loud, "Forget it." After all, there was no one on the street to hear me muttering to myself. "I will use my quarter to buy myself a cup of coffee at the all-night diner near home." Which, not surprisingly, considering how the whole sorry affair had evolved, was closed for repairs.

By the time I got home, I was so wet and miserable that the dog took pity on me. For the first and only time, I actually made it past the trigger step without setting him off!

The girl never even called to thank me for a swell evening.

I began to give serious thought to a drastic behavioral makeover. Maybe no more booze. Possibly no more dating. Then I thought better of it. I would simply exercise better judgment from that moment on.

I clearly remember promising my brother never to tell our parents that he was the culprit, not some hit and run driver, who put the dent in the rear bumper of Mom's new car. We were at Jones Beach, and he backed into a post while parking. Although he bribed me with an ice cream float, that wasn't enough.

"You'd better be really nice to me from now on, or I will tell Mom what happened here."

Bold words from a ten-year-old to his much bigger brother. But I had the upper hand, and I played it for all it was worth.

I am going to call him up any time now and remind him that I kept my word, whereas he did not. He should have come over to Trude Heller's and bailed me out. Maybe quote Marlon Brando, speaking to Rod Steiger in that famous taxicab scene from *On the Waterfront*. "You was my brother... You shoulda looked out for me a little bit. You shoulda taken care of me just a little bit." Probably, I'll skip that part about nearly being a contender.

Maybe, just maybe, I should have kept a twenty-dollar bill in my sock. For an emergency.

Because "You never know, my little Rosanne Rosanna Danna."

Nice Try

'Twas a few nights before Christmas, and, as usual, I was in a panic. Had I been living in a big city, there wouldn't have been much of a problem. But this was small-town America, and, other than drug stores and Fred Meyer, options were few. This was last century. Before Jeff Bezos had sold a single book out of his garage.

I lay in bed wracking my brains, but the grey matter resisted cooperating to the max. All I could think about was Christmas carols. Mentally, I scrolled through the list of every carol I could think of, hoping with this diversion to clear the memory banks enough to turn to the task ahead: what to put under the tree this year.

"Deck the Halls" made me feel bad that I had no holly, just a few rather worn artificial garlands. On the other hand, "It Came Upon a Midnight Clear" was the possible harbinger of an epiphany. Wearying, instead of counting sheep to lull myself to sleep, I went through "The Twelve Days of Christmas" backwards. It's a holiday substitute for the cognitive test of counting back from one hundred by sevens, which I sincerely doubt was asked of Donald Trump.

Behold, I had my revelation!

"Do you sell partridges here?"

The Astoria, Oregon, pet store owner looked at me incredulously. Astoria has only 10,000 or so human inhabitants. There may, in fact, be a few partridges in the wilds of Clatsop County, but none were to be had at that time, or any other time, at the pet store.

"The F5 Ranch in Prineville may have some frozen chukar partridge breasts."

"Prineville is way far away, and anyway I was looking for a pet partridge."

"Why would you want a pet partridge?"

"To go with my pear tree." Actually, I had not committed to buying the pear tree yet, but I had the nursery on my list. The clerk didn't get the point. I didn't bother explaining.

"Okay. Well, what birds do you have?"

"I have a nice cockatiel, a mynah, some canaries, and parakeets..."

My father used to keep parakeets in his office. He always would take them home over the holidays. If they survived the benign neglect we gave them, he would take them back to his office in January. Whatever. They never seemed to last long. Yet, undeterred, he always came back the following year with new ones.

"...And I have a few finches."

Bingo! Since I hadn't purchased the pear tree yet, I came up with a new plan. I would buy a nice *Ficus*. We had space for a little tree in the living room.

"I'll take a finch."

"You can't buy just one finch."

"Why not?"

"Because it will die of boredom."

"You serious?"

"There are only two things that will kill a finch in a cage."

Oh, I forgot. *I needed a cage, too.* He happened to have a few for sale.

"You mean, besides old age?"

"Well, that, too. The main things that get them, though, are boredom and a chill." He has me thinking, *We might have left Dad's parakeets too close to an open window.*

"Okay then. I will take two finches and a cage. And some of whatever it is that finches eat.

I stashed the finches in the office, turned the heat up, and dashed over to the nursery to buy a *Ficus*. The only one they had was seven feet tall.

"Don't you have a smaller one?"

"Not until April."

I was desperate, so I bought what he had and lugged it over to the office.

Christmas morning, I excused myself after breakfast and opening the stocking stuffers. I returned with the goods. The tree was hanging out of the back window, which I kept rolled up as far as I could, so the finches wouldn't get chilled and die before I got them into the house.

The kids were excited. My wife was not amused. The proverbial stink eye was cast in my direction.

"What the hell is all this?"

"Oh, you know, two finches and a fig tree."

"I can see that. Where are they going? And who is going to take care of them?"

I will have you know that I have had some considerable success in caring for animals by myself.

In boarding school, my roommate and I kept a dog in our room for three months, feeding him everything but dog food. His favorite food was doughnuts, by the way. We called him Little Nort, after Big Nort, who was our favorite math teacher. Sadly, his owners happened to find him one day, as he and I were doing some business in the woods. Actually, he was doing his business, and I was searching for a quiet place to take my date for the upcoming prom, ostensibly for a view of the Milky Way.

And that is not all. I had a cat with me for a semester, senior year at Yale. Scarlett O'Hara was probably unhappy about his name, but that was his problem. My problem was that he would lie in wait for me until I got back from a long day of classes and Glee Club practice. It would be fangs, teeth and fur flying as soon as I got in the door. We would wrestle for a while until the blood loss was excessive, whereupon I would staunch the hemorrhage and feed him real cat food instead of human flesh (mine) There would be an uneasy truce for the rest of the evening and night.

But wait; there is more. In medical school, I kept a frog in my dorm room through the winter. He survived Physiology Lab, because I could not pith him {Look up the word; it might come in handy in conversation. You never know.}. Instead, I zipped him into my coat pocket and beat a hasty retreat to the exit. He ate some of almost anything he was given and let the rest rot in his little fishbowl cum terrarium, which I assiduously cleaned every six weeks or so, followed by exercising him in the hallway, to the delight of one tree-hugging classmate from

Wyoming, who was more used to animals than humans, for obvious reasons.

"Of course, I will take care of the finches. And I will water the fig tree. Even though they are your Christmas present."

"Why did you buy this stuff?" The older kids were clued in. They started singing the pertinent Christmas carol, and she got the point.

"Ha-ha."

The kids told all their friends. My wife told no one. Not even her younger sister, to whom she always had told everything. Until that point.

My parents came out for a visit. Dad asked, "What's wrong with parakeets?"

Mom, who always liked things just so, remarked, "My, they are messy little things. Who cleans up after them?"

We planned a vacation and asked the office staff to take care of the birds while we were gone. So back they went to the office.

When we returned, one of the birds was gone to bird heaven.

"What happened?"

"I don't know. They seemed fine on Friday evening."

"You didn't turn the heat off, did you?"

"I always do, over the weekend."

I took the survivor home and told my wife I was going back to the pet shop to buy another finch.

"Why on earth would you want to bring another messy

bird into the house? You already had your little Christmas joke. If you buy another bird, I am leaving." One of the little girls started to cry.

That was my chance, but I didn't act on it. Instead, I had another epiphany.

"Whatever do you want a compact for?"

I removed the little mirror and affixed it to the inside of the cage. It worked splendidly. The lone survivor thought there was two of him (or her, or them) and remained fully engaged. I made sure to keep the room temperature nice and toasty.

Until the day the bird passed on. But not from boredom. Or the chill. It simply was his (or her, or their) time.

Anybody need a slightly-used bird cage? Or a nine-foot *Ficus*?

Peripatetic

{From the Greek peripatētikos *'walking up and down'; walking about, while discoursing, in the manner of Socrates}*

In 2019, the last full year when we were free to go most anywhere without recourse to social distancing or the wearing of masks, I averaged 4,770 steps a day. Last year, I was up to 7,544. So far this year, through mid-June, I am logging in 10,267. I know this because I carry my smart phone with me, and it keeps track of all sorts of statistics, some of them actually useful.

I am aiming for over 11,000/ day, but life keeps getting in the way of walking.

Our late, lamented rescue dog, minette, a Havanese/ poodle mix, enjoyed her walks, but not to the extent of Louis le Premier du Lac. Louis is a chihuahua/ Italian greyhound mélange. He joined the family in August and took full control by September. Louis seems to know no limit when it comes to walking, unless it is raining cats and dogs. Hence the noticeable uptick in steps.

Mary almost always comes with us, which emphasizes the second half of the definition above. Mind you, it is possible to carry on a one-sided conversation with one's dog while ambulating. I do this frequently, especially when nobody else is within earshot. Louis appears to understand much of what I say, so long as I do not mumble.

But to be sure, he gains more intellectual stimulation from his nose than from his ears, which can be frustrating when attempting to cover more ground in less time. I try not to take personally any inattention on his part.

With Mary in attendance, conversation becomes distinctly more meaningful. It's the give and take of it all. On the other hand, I have to be more measured in my words. Mary is more capable of taking exception to a remark that I might care to make than is Louis. If I cross a certain line, Mary sullenly might suggest that I change the subject, which I am quite certain Louis would never presume to hint at. It would seem too much like biting the hand that feeds one, a thing one ought never to contemplate, no matter how annoying the conversation.

When I indicated that I carry my smart phone with me, I do not mean to suggest that I use it while walking dog, wife, or both, other than to track steps. In fact, it is almost always set on "Do Not Disturb," which my daughters find frustrating, but which they grudgingly concede is my prerogative.

And, why, you might ask, do I not refer frequently, if not incessantly, to my phone while ambulating, like so many members of the younger generations one finds around in ever-increasing, often irritating numbers? Alternatively, why not rely upon earbuds to cocoon oneself in a cradle of constant auditory gratification?

Here are but a few reasons:

1. My dogs have cultivated the habit of crisscrossing in front of me wherever they go, and an errant foot placement on my part might, at least, cause distress and, at most, cause permanent damage, either to the dog or to me.

2. That above-mentioned errant foot placement might result in a heel-full or more of excrement. Back in the good old days, when soles were simple, a quick wipe on a patch of grass sufficed. My father often resorted to that remedy. Now that we favor complex tread patterns on our footwear, pressure washing and scraping with plastic knives or screwdrivers are required for adequate removal of unwanted accretions.

3. I prefer to know who is ahead and hope to have some inkling of what is coming up behind me, so that I can move or leap out of harm's way, whether that comes in the form of a virus, a runner, or a rapid conveyance.

4. Mary would be likely to take offence, were I to whip out the phone in the midst of a discussion, unless I were first to seek her permission, say to settle an argument before descending to the level of name-calling.

5. There are such an abundance of interesting types of fauna and flora out there. Beavers, herons, eagles, coyotes, the odd cougar. You wouldn't think, right here in Seattle...

6. There also is a profusion of different license plates in our neck of the woods. Vanity plates, out of state plates, cheap non-embossed plates. Over the past year, we have identified vehicles from every state in the Union but Rhode Island.

7. We remain vigilant, looking for a sign from Above. Problem is, if you keep your eyes peeled on High, so as to be sure of not missing an omen, you run the risk of walking into a tree. Which, in itself, is a sign that you are spending far too much time with your head in the clouds, as it were.

8. We certainly wouldn't want to miss all the quirky goings on in the neighborhood.

I will stop right there and clarify. On the corner, by the turn into our parking lot, lurked a fellow named Robert who fervently believed that Satan lives in the cell phone. Legend has it that he once accosted a man who was innocently attempting to tell his wife that he might be a bit late to dinner. This, indeed, turned out to be prophetic, as the police were summoned, and an ambulance dispatched following the altercation.

Robert's Prozac dosage was adjusted, and thereafter he was frequently seen directing traffic that was not there and conversing with phantoms in a distinctly non-philosophical way. Ostensibly rendered harmless with industrial quantities of psychotropic medications. Still, it generally was considered hazardous to approach the corner with a cell phone in hand.

Strange as it may seem, Robert was the caretaker for someone else, a recluse. Irene owned the house, and Robert lived in the basement. He would post warnings about demons on his windows and occasionally would tack lengthy, handwritten stream-of-consciousness notes on the corner power pole.

When Irene died, her house went to Robert, who preferred not to continue to live there—a decision that was greatly appreciated by the entire community. Instead, he donated the house to the Salvation Army, which sold the property to a developer who, in turn, tore the place down and put up four condos. So it goes.

Although Robert is long gone, those of us who had some knowledge of him still think twice about talking on our phones as we approach his corner. I guess it represents a nod of sorts to his memory, or perhaps it is nothing more than a matter of ingrained habituation.

Then there is Mike, the "Emperor of Eastlake." You wouldn't guess that he had been anointed or appointed, if you kept your head buried in your phone while walking by his place. But the title is there in plain sight, above the driver's side door of his unique imperial chariot. Visualize the front end of a VW beetle, soldered to a motorcycle, and you pretty much have got what I am getting at.

He also sports a second VW beetle, this one two-toned, with Demolition Derby-size tires. Also a vintage Caddy in considerably less than pristine condition, festooned with longhorns in front and metal testicles in the back.

Mike can be found at almost any daylight hour surveying his realm from a lounge chair on his front lawn. There is an abundance of seasonally-adjusted amusements set out for his immediate pleasure: a pool table, more or less leveled to his sloping lawn; a corrugated tub of water, large enough for bathing a bird or a small dog, or for doing water aerobics, one ankle at a time; a diminutive swing set for dolls or squirrels; a freeform outdoor barbecue, meaning coals in a pile on the grass. The beer cooler seems to be a permanent fixture, as are the more-than-slightly-damaged blue marlin trophy and the wooden cutout of Eloise.

Hailing from New York, well aware of the delightful tales of the impish, irrepressible Eloise, and finding her full-length graven image on Mike's lawn a bit incongruous, I stopped in my tracks and humbly approached the Emperor.

"Do you know what you have there?" Perhaps I should have added, "Excellency." Yet, there was something about his dirty feet and the "10-4, good buddy" T-shirt that put me off full obeisance.

"Yeah. It's Eloise."

"Have you read any of the books about her?"

"Nah. I just saw this thing at some guy's house, thought it was kind of cool, and bought it from him."

If you are the Emperor, why not simply appropriate it? I thought, but instead offered him my vintage Space Jam T-shirt in trade. For a fleeting moment, he seemed tempted. Unfortunately, he declined. It seems that I may need to sweeten the pot, if I ever hope to wrest Eloise from Mike.

Merely two blocks from the Empire is the outdoor abode of one Peapod Hieronymus. I say outdoor, because she is perpetually in situ, whenever I walk by, from morning to night, April through November. Her whereabouts during the dreary, colder months are perplexing. Some say she migrates; others contend she dematerializes. Absolutely no one can offer any explanation for her name.

On the other side of the street, raw meat occasionally can be seen hanging from trees, seemingly with neither rhyme nor apparent reason. This is always well in advance of the holiday season and is distinctly different from a Christmas ornament. I thought, *Perhaps it was intended as a feeder for vultures or condors,* but all I ever saw was a horde of flies. I wondered whether *It might be an offering to some god or other.* Fascinated though repelled, I tracked the longevity of this unique tree adornment for some five or six days, until it disappeared as mysteriously as it had manifested. I asked Peapod about this.

"Yeah, well, they hang up stuff like that once or twice a year."

"What do they do with it?"

"Dunno. It seems to harden before they take it down. Kind of like jerky. I think maybe they eat it."

In between these real originals {cf. *Cool Hand Luke,*

when George Kennedy says to Paul Newman, "You is a real original."} is the awesome horticultural corner of Another Mary. Not my Mary, who leaves all plant care to me. This corner denizen transformed the space in the course of one year into a marvel of urban flora, at what I am sure has been considerable cost.

Her largesse in beautifying the neighborhood extends even to those who are too cheap, lazy, dishonest, or all of the above to buy their roses from the Eastlake Flower Lady shop. I have seen them swing by in broad daylight, roll down their car window, pull out shears, and snip off a bouquet of roses, despite my voluble remonstrances. Had my head been in my cell phone, I might have missed such outrageous larceny. I nearly always photograph the license and notify the local constabulary, who, their hands full dealing with protestors, arsonists, anarchists, reporters, videographers, rubberneckers, and the ACLU, politely brush me off.

Undaunted, Another Mary keeps tending the rose bushes, while growing fabulous dahlias, gardenias, hydrangeas, Japanese maples, and the like. Her work extended across the street until a mega-housing development put an end to her expansion. My Mary and I certainly do enjoy smelling her roses, those that are spared the untimely and unsolicited shearing thereof.

We vary our routes, depending upon the time of day, weather conditions, and the whim and fancy of Louis, who generally prefers to take the lead. Wherever we end up, all we have to say to Louis is, "Take us home," and he does so, unfailingly. Even from a variety of points as far as two miles away.

He tried this on his own once. Louis managed to squirm out of his halter and took off for home, with me in hot pursuit. The Italian greyhound in him renders it impossible for me to catch him, unless he is of a mind to let me do so, which he only will do in our co-op parking lot.

Over a mile from home, it was a different story. Louis paused a number of times, as I chased behind, just long enough for me to get close before scampering off. Next thing, he was in rush-hour traffic on our busiest neighborhood two-way thoroughfare, racing for his life down the median, until a car slowed enough for him to cross and continue his journey home. A kind passerby managed to corral him on a side street until I caught up, and all was well. But nearly not.

Louis has been quite the needy little fellow ever since. That experience seems to have chastened him.

During the short days of winter in our northerly clime, we often are out after dark. Mary has purchased all manner of glowing collars, reflective sashes, flashing lights, and neon hats to save our necks.

The main problem, however, day or night, especially in the cold weather, is fogging of the eyeglasses. That and tearing. And runny noses. Masks really are a pain, although undeniably critical in coronavirus control. I have taken to walking without glasses, which is less risky than trying to see anything through the fog. This works well enough in daylight, but not great at night. We deal with it.

One of our routes takes us by an older fellow who has been building an MGB out of junkyard parts, in his garage. At the beginning of the pandemic, he started with nothing more than a bare chassis. Gradually he added panels, axles, wheels, seats, wiring, hood, trunk, tires, dashboard, steering wheel, windshield, engine, and convertible top, more or less in that order. Sanded down the spare parts and painted the car forest green. Did every bit of the work himself.

Building a car is one thing. Getting in and out of bucket seats is another. This car, he tells me, is going to his grandson.

Just beyond him is a woman who maintains a miniature gnome landscape that features timely holiday and seasonal variations. We have admired elaborate setups for Valentine's and St. Patrick's Days, Easter, the Fourth of July, Halloween, Thanksgiving, and Christmas. I take photos of each new display and dutifully email them to my four- and seven-year-old English granddaughters, who have yet to comment on them. Maybe their parents don't show them the shots, because they are afraid that gnomes will creep them out. I don't ask; they don't tell. I just keep sending more photos.

Kind of like *Amélie*, if you remember the title character's weird and wonderful affinity for postal-card photos from all of her travels, always featuring her gnome in the foreground. Her efforts, too, appeared to come to naught, if I recall correctly. But, in the end, everything worked out.

Eventually, the grandkids will get their own cell phones. I wouldn't be at all surprised if they start photographing any gnomes they happen upon, too. Maybe they will send the photos to me.

I could go on, but it's time for another family walk. As usual, we will let Louis take us wherever he feels like going, as long as he stays on his leash. Who knows where he might take us? Who knows what we might see?

"Just Around the Corner, There's a Rainbow in the Sky…"

{Full disclosure: I believe in miracles. And angels. And past life regression. Karma, too. I believe there is a purpose for everything. I do not believe in coincidences.}

"Let's take a nap after lunch. We can take our long walk afterwards."

As I already indicated, we do a lot of walking. More this year than last. I know that I am more fit than last year, because my wife tells me so. Thank you, COVID-19, for that much.

Thank you as well to ZsaZsa, who we believe brought minette to us, and to minette for allowing Louis le Premier du Lac to come into our life. One at a time, these little souls in fur suits commandeered a piece of prime real estate in our hearts, as only dogs can do. Each of them in their own way. Each of them wonderfully.

Louis is our fitness motivator. He picked right up where minette left off, brought us out of our doldrums, and kicks our butts all over three neighborhoods. He may be nearly ten, but he has something not unlike puppy energy that keeps him going, rainy days excepted.

"Honey, the rain has stopped, and I believe I can see a glimpse of blue in the sky. Let's go now, and maybe nap later." Discussions like this would never have come up before the pandemic, but we all have plenty of time on our hands these days, and naps have become essential aids in filling the time.

"Okay, but just a short walk." Short for Louis can be as much as an hour, unless it is mealtime.

We are starting to think about leaving him behind for gradually increasing periods, in preparation for the fact that the pandemic actually might end someday, as theaters, restaurants, gyms, sport arenas—places where Louis is not allowed—once again might become viable options. But, not yet. For now, wherever we go, he goes.

So, off we went, on this particular day. As usual, we let Louis lead us. He often varies his route, according to some inscrutable, trailblazing gene. On a good day, I can influence the critical decision-making that occurs primarily at street corners. Most of the time, I don't bother. He always seems to have a plan.

I should mention that Louis was just coming off a couple of bad days: agitated in the middle of the night; pooping on the carpet; throwing up on the bed, on a different carpet, and on our newly-upholstered white denim sofa. He hadn't eaten in two days. Or, perhaps more accurately, nothing he had eaten stayed with him.

He had become increasingly reluctant to eat. On more than one occasion, we had to resort to spoon-feeding him. Mary kept remarking that he didn't seem to like his current brand as much as what he previously had been used to.

We realized, to our horror, that we had been feeding the poor dog cat food. For a month. Six pounds of it! It was bad enough that, for the first few weeks he was with us, we persisted in referring to Louis as "she," following as he did in the pawsteps of ZsaZsa and minette. Now we were disrespecting, not only his gender, but his species.

Organic, dried, grain-free cat food often is packaged in a container that is quite similar to its canine equivalent. Admittedly, the one carries a rather subdued image of a cat, down in a lower corner, whereas the other subtly displays a generic pooch. And the word "cat," or "dog" actually may be discovered in small print on the box, should one scrutinize the text as thoroughly as if it were the Talmud.

To be sure, we are not talking "Little Friskies" versus "Alpo" here. Shopping at the holistic pet food boutique requires a higher than garden variety of perceptive skill. One towards which we only now are beginning to aspire.

Indeed, the contents of these high-end pet foods differ only in proportion and in the all-important feline additive of an abundance of spinach, which does not agree with dogs. Especially after the attempted digestion, albeit gradual, of six pounds of cat food. Hence Louis' two-day sinking spell. There plainly is a limit to how much cat food a dog can take without adverse effects, and Louis had reached it.

This whole thing was pretty upsetting. Louis had become as weak as a kitten.

Which is why we felt the walk should be short. That and the fact that we are cranky if we don't get our nap.

Louis had other ideas. He summoned up an extra ounce of energy from deep within his nine-pound self and took us on a lengthy tour of one quadrant of the city, including a few parts hitherto unknown. This we did not mind, because it was unseasonably warm, and the combination of sun and clouds provided gorgeous dramatic lighting. Chiaroscuro. Nature imitating Caravaggio and Rembrandt.

The sun stays quite low in the sky during late December in Seattle, that is, if you are fortunate enough to see the sun at all. Friends back East find it surprising to hear that Seattle is as far north as Newfoundland—also, for that matter, that King County is as big as Connecticut, if you count Lake Washington and Elliott Bay. For them, Seattle is all about Microsoft, Amazon, Boeing—and the rain. I do try to inculcate them with a few other pithy pearls of knowledge about the place. For example: Bigfoot, Nirvana, and Rainier beer.

Lo and behold, Louis, as if on a mission, took us over a hill to a place from which we gazed east across Portage Bay to view the brightest, most vivid rainbow either of us ever had seen. He walked another block or two with us in tow, then headed up a steep incline and stopped, perhaps to sniff, or maybe it was to indulge us, as we struggled to catch our breaths. We looked north and found the other end of the rainbow, equally vivid. We were more or less dragged up another block, where we could now visualize the whole rainbow, sporting a double rainbow at one end!

{*A digression on rainbows in the manner of Melville, who frequently interrupts the story line of* Moby Dick *to add a point or twenty-five of expostulation upon the scientific study of whales.*}

Rainbows are formed when light emerges from water droplets that are in just the right place for the rays to enter our eyes. Such droplets always lie on a circle facing the Sun. Unless we're airborne, or on top of a mountain while looking at a climber atop a nearby peak—when a rainbow can mimic a halo, hence called "a glory"—we can only see a "bow," as the ground blocks out the rest.

We actually saw of one of these optical phenomena

from the sky, on our way to Alaska. Sadly, our camera was not at the ready. {There are several fabulous images that can be Googled. Simply type in the words "rainbow" and "glory." Several display a double, full-circle rainbow, which is what we were fortunate enough to see.}

The double rainbow effect, though uncommon, is noteworthy on several accounts: the second rainbow is invariably fainter; it has nearly twice the width of the primary one; the colors are reversed.

Logically, a triple rainbow would be fainter still, likely fatter, and would display colors in the same order as the primary rainbow. I am pretty sure that I witnessed this phenomenon once, in Astoria, OR, where it rains far more and far harder than Seattle. So hard that people have been known to see things, like Japanese submarines in the Columbia River. According to the Optical Society in Washington, D.C.—a scientific society with 16,000 members around the world—there have been only five scientific reports of triple rainbows in 250 years, rendering a two-headed heifer more common.

Rainbows are particularly meaningful to Mary and me. We have had a painting of one hanging on the wall for our entire marriage. After ZsaZsa died, transient rainbows appeared, seemingly out of nowhere, on the floor of our apartment and our floating home, within minutes of minette's first visit to each place. Since then, they never have reappeared in the same places. We interpreted these signs as a welcoming from one departed dog, transformed into an angel, to her successor.

When Louis first came to us, a similar scenario played itself out. Make that two angels.

Had we taken that nap, or had we insisted on a short walk, we never would have been in a position to witness this marvel of nature. And Louis might have come home as sick as ever. Instead, we believe that ZsaZsa and minette interceded to convince Louis that he indeed is every bit a dog, a male one at that, and that his chances of resolution of his intestinal miseries now approached 100%.

Louis brought us home directly from the rainbow and gobbled up his dinner. The right stuff. And kept it down.

VI. Thus and So

{"…So, let's have another cup o' coffee…"}

"...And Let's Have Another Piece o' Pie!"

Towards the end of her life, after she had managed to get past serious health and alcohol addiction issues, my mother found routines to be comforting. Every morning, she would eat a bowl of Kellogg's Special K cereal, which represented a big shift for her, as she had, for years before that, started every morning with corn flakes. Every evening she would have fresh shrimp salad, which Dad would pick up for her that day at the fish market in Wayne, New Jersey, where he worked the till.

A comedown after retiring from a successful practice of pediatrics in New York City, you say. I can assure you that the proprietor loved to tell his customers, after wrapping up their order: "You go right over to Dr. Weber there. He will take your money." The truth is that Dad was never in it for the money—neither in medicine, nor in fish marketing. He was just happy for something to do in the daytime, until the Mets came on TV. There he was, running the cash register and chatting up everybody who came in the store.

His pay? All the fish he and mom could eat. For mom that was shrimp salad, topped off with a nice piece of apple pie. Never cherry, pecan, or lemon meringue (my personal favorites, in case you ever invite me to dinner).

A sizeable number of those who get past their addiction

to alcohol turn to smoking. Not my mother. She began to collect Kleenex boxes. After she died, I discovered an entire bathroom cabinet filled with Kleenex containers of all sizes. It appeared as though she was seeking out every available color and design.

I guess I inherited the collecting gene from both my parents, although it was Dad who really got me started. When I was a little kid, he started purchasing mint sheets of stamps, which he put into albums for my brother and me. He did this for nine or ten years. He was convinced that mint sheets would be a better long-term investment than single stamps, first day covers (specially designed envelopes for first day of issue stamps), or plate blocks (four attached stamps bearing a unique mint number at the margin).

I never caught the mint sheet bug, although I retained Dad's albums. I did start a collection of single U.S. stamps, mostly unused. This was my hobby through grade school and well into high school. Dad helped me along by buying a few high-end items that I could not afford on my allowance.

Oh, I collected lots of other things, too: *Mad Magazines*, baseball cards, 45 rpm records. I never lost interest in baseball, but I stopped collecting cards after accumulating full sets from 1957- 60. Sadly, they found their way to the trash barrel before I went off to college. Not my choice, but, oh well. Same thing for the *Mad Magazines* and the old 45s. I can only imagine what 200 vintage 45s from

'57- 62 would go for today on eBay. Or those full sets of baseball cards. Or my *Mad* collection, for that matter.

As if that wasn't enough, I began to collect foreign coins. For my eighth birthday, my parents gave me a "Coins of the World" album, with slots for a coin from each of 150 or so countries. A significant part of my allowance over the ensuing five years found its way into the hands of various dealers, as I tracked down one representative coin from each of the countries.

I filled up that album, put it aside for forty years—perhaps looking at it twice in all that time—and gave it to one of my daughters. She, in turn, will pass it on to her son. He will find, if and when he looks, that some of the countries with slots in that old album have changed their names. A number no longer exist. And so it goes.

I found it more appealing to collect U.S. coins, most of which I found by combing through pocket change and by exchanging greenbacks for coins at our savings bank. In those days, you could still find silver dollars in stores and at banks.

Mercury dimes and liberty walking half dollars were still in wide circulation. Indian head pennies, buffalo nickels, and standing liberty quarters, although more uncommon, also were to be found. Net result, I got a good start on all these varieties of coinage.

The harder I studied in high school and especially in college, the less time I had for numismatics and philately.

Yet, collector to the core as I am, I managed to hold on to my stamp and coin albums. Neglected although retained, in the sure and certain hope of a resurrection.

John Macurdy, a leading *basso* at the Metropolitan Opera in NYC, was invited to sing in the 1985-7 Seattle *Ring* cycles. As soon as I heard that, I pulled some strings and got the word to him that I had followed his career for 30 years—from his early years as a chorister and soloist at my church in NYC, through his operatic career—and inquired whether he might like a nice, home-cooked meal. He told me that he would love that.

Thus, began a friendship. Dinners together, at my place and his in Stamford, CT. Backstage visits at Seattle Opera and at the Met. And stamp collecting. His active interest in that hobby revived mine.

Everyone specializes one way or another in their philatelic pursuits, for example: U.S. 19th century, Airmail, Special Delivery, Postage Due, Department of Revenue, Migratory Bird Hunting, or error stamps; international endangered animals, British colonial, or triangular stamps. John specialized in the 1851 one-cent Ben Franklin issue, of which he had dozens. Talk about focusing!

I remember him telling me that he was planning to sell his collection. "They're only paper, after all, and paper will disintegrate, sooner or later." This was a bit of a revelation to me. Especially when delivered in his authoritative, booming bass voice.

That was one reason I switched back to numismatics.

The other was that the best part of my stamp collection mysteriously disappeared in 2004.

Coin collecting is a bit harder to explain to the uninitiated. While stamps offer a panoply of gorgeous images and colors, as well as a vast array of historic evocations, coins can be a monotonous lot. To most, an album of Roosevelt dimes is of next to no interest. What do they know about a 1982, no mint mark? Do they even know what mint marks signify? To them, a nice, shiny 2021 dime looks better than a shopworn 1948.

You can take out a magnifying glass and show them the tiny "V.B.D." initials on the reverse of a 1909 S Lincoln penny, and they will say something like, "What's so special, if you can hardly see them?" You can explain things like supply and demand until you are blue in the face. You can show them an example of toning (rainbow coloration at the edges), or a valuable, if somewhat dirty-looking piece, and they will ask why you don't simply clean it up. They simply do not understand.

On the other hand, show them the 1935 National Parks series of stamps, which, sadly, I no longer can do, except in photographs, and they will say, "How pretty!" That they are. Not particularly valuable, but lovely to look at.

There is no doubt that the standing liberty quarter and the liberty walking half dollar are beautiful coins. Yet, many would ask, "Why collect more than one of each type, when they are all look the same?" Stated differently, "See one, seen them all."

Those who give the matter any thought may wonder why a numismatist would ever bother to open their safe deposit box just to pore over a complete set of, say, Morgan dollars, only to lock it up again. I must confess that the pursuit of the harder-to-get, more valuable coins—those that bedevil routine attempts to fill the few remaining slots in an album—is more thrilling than looking at the filled pages of the finished product. The casual observer will find it considerably more interesting to leaf through a stamp album, if nothing else, to chart the inexorable increase in postage fees through the years.

Since 1892, the U.S. Mint has offered an alternative for those who prefer variety in their coin collection, and that is an extensive series of commemorative issues. They are intended for collectors and, as such, rarely, if ever, find their way into circulation, although they are legal tender. Most are quite beautiful reminders of important aspects of our national history.

Beginning in 1999 with statehood commemoration, followed by a national parks series, variations in the reverse of the circulated Washington quarter became the norm. In 2004-5 the nickel featured four different reverse designs and a new image of Jefferson on the obverse. The penny in 2009 featured four different phases of Lincoln's life. The Presidential dollar series from 2007-16, the Native American dollar, with a new reverse each year beginning in 2009, and the Innovation dollar, dating from 2018, with four different images a year, are all to be found in circulation, although not widely used. All of these issues show the Mint is making an effort to vary its circulating coinage, adding the element of commemoration, and thereby decreasing the monotony.

There are those who succumb to the collecting bug, as an investment, or a hobby, or both. Not necessarily for stamps or coins—perhaps for, say, works of art, rare books, antique wicker, or various and sundry items like salt and pepper shakers, Beanie Babies, vintage sneakers, etc. Some search high-end galleries, others frequent garage sales and flea markets, especially as pandemic restrictions are beginning to lessen. And some could care less.

Just remember that, "One man's piece of junk is another man's treasure." It's the aphorism that eBay depends upon.

Hyperbole

A man walks into a bar with his dog...

We were visiting Dad daily in a four-bed, semi-intensive care unit at NYU Medical Center. One of the other patients in the room looked to be in pretty bad shape, which is generally a requirement for entry into such a setting. The fact is, he was suffering from severe pancreatitis, a life-threatening condition.

His wife was there at his bedside every time we came

by. After a few days, we got to chatting a bit. Dad's surgeon had just come by to check on him.

"Sounds like your father is getting better," she offered.

"Yes, thank God, it seems so. How about your husband? How is he doing?"

"Well, I really don't know. He has been here for twelve days." And she shocks us by adding, "I haven't seen his doctor."

"Really? Did you ask the nurses to tell him to talk to you?"

"Certainly. I was hoping that he would stop by while I was here."

"You certainly seem to be putting in long hours at his bedside."

"Oh yes. I get here first thing in the morning and I stay until visiting hours are over." That amounted to thirteen hours a day.

"And you mean to tell me, in all that time, he never came by to see your husband?"

"Sometimes an intern or a resident drops by, but they are always in such a hurry. They rush in with a nurse and a trayful of syringes, ask who gets what, administer the medications, and off they go."

"Have you told one of them that you would like to see the man in charge?"

"Yes, but they always tell me how busy he is."

"You don't seem particularly upset about this lack of communication."

"I'm not. Everyone says he is **the best**."

"My dog can talk!"
"Dogs cannot talk," says the bartender.
"If I can get him to talk, will you give me
a free beer?"
"Why not?"

My uncle was a well-respected ear, nose, and throat specialist. In fact, he did consultations for Presidents Kennedy, Johnson, and Nixon. Although he never thought of himself as a surgeon, he did operate on LBJ. No, not to take out his gall bladder (Remember when LBJ pulled up his shirt and displayed his abdominal scar, in a crass display of tastelessness?). My uncle removed some nasal polyps. And they must have been some whoppers, considering the size of that schnozz and the fact that it was grown in Texas, where everything is **the biggest, if not the best.**

"Fido, what's on top of a building?"
"Ruuf!"

Uncle died at the age of 74. I believe that his life might have been prolonged, had his wife, herself a nurse, called 911 instead of his personal cardiologist, whose office was five crowded miles of New York City streets away. The man came by ASAP, but not soon enough, little black bag in hand, did an exam and proceeded to argue with my uncle for fifteen minutes about the advisability of his going to the hospital. And then drove him there, where he had a cardiac arrest almost immediately upon entering the emergency room.

At no time was an ambulance called! Therefore, he was deprived of timely critical interventions, such as oxygen and intravenous medications. Yet, my aunt believed until the day she died that "They did everything they could." But mostly that the cardiologist she called was **the best**.

> Bartender: "Stop wasting my time."
> Man: "I guarantee he talks. Let me ask him something else. Fido, tell us the consistency of sandpaper."
> Dog: "Ruff!!"

Dad was told to show up for admission to the hospital by 9 a.m. the day before his aneurysm surgery. We had driven him in from New Jersey.

"Sorry, the room is not ready yet. Check with us in an hour."

The waiting area was jam-packed, but at least he found a seat. Four hours later, I told the lady that I was taking him out to lunch.

After lunch, same story. No room.

After dinner, ditto.

He wasn't admitted until 11:30 that night! He was exhausted from all the hours of waiting. I was livid.

"Dad, why didn't you let that New Jersey surgeon do your surgery closer to home? There would have been so much less hassle."

You know the answer, without my telling you.

"This is ridiculous."

*"One more question, please. He talks, I tell you. Fido, tell us who was **the best** baseball player of all time."*

"Ruth!!!"

Maybe the pendulum is swinging the other way. Parents, teachers, coaches have started rewarding kids for simply participating. Forget striving to be **the best**. You get a trophy just for showing up. Even if you don't make much of an effort.

> *The man and his dog have been kicked out of the bar. The man is sitting on the curb, holding his head in his hands, shaking his head in disbelief. "This is nuts. I can't understand it."*
>
> *The dog walks up to him, wagging his tail: "DiMaggio?"*

Here is where I take exception. Ty Cobb may well have been **the best**. You can look up his stats and make up your own mind. Okay, so he was a little crazy. Babe Ruth was not exactly what you would call normal. Joe Di Maggio was crazy, too—crazy about Marilyn Monroe.

Let me ask you this: who has the right to determine who is **the best** anyway? Okay, say in a math test, there you can accurately quantify. But **the best** essay (aside from this one)? **The best** Downward Facing Dog? **The best** underwater basket-weaving course?

The best baseball player? Come on. There were hundreds of good ones. Over 19,000 have played Major League baseball, including Eddie Gaedel, who is on the list for a single appearance at bat. He popped out of a cake in full uniform (all three-and-a-half feet of him), was inserted into the lineup as a pinch hitter, ordered not to swing, walked on four pitches, and immediately was replaced with a pinch runner. One could argue that he was **the best** professional-baseball-playing midget.

Now let me ask you: What does being **the best** get you? Ty Cobb ended up a lonely old man, sleeping every night with his Coca Cola stock certificates and a handgun under his pillow. Bobby Fischer, **the best** chess player of his time, ended up persona non grata in the U.S. and lived out the last three years of his life in Iceland. Muhammed Ali, **the self-proclaimed greatest**, landed in jail. John Lennon ended up assassinated. So did Lincoln. Mozart may well have been poisoned. I will not belabor the point.

Mark McGuire certainly was a gifted baseball player. Big and strong, he was a prolific hitter. His problem was that he wanted to be **the best**. Better than Babe Ruth. He bulked up on anabolic steroids, which increased his strength and his bat speed. His 70 home runs set a single season record, breaking the old record by 9. Which doesn't really count, because he cheated.

Barry Bonds wanted to do him a few better. Unlike McGuire, he was a great all-around baseball player, well on his way to a Hall of Fame career. Yet he, too, wanted to be **the best**. In his mind, that meant better than McGuire. So, he cheated, too. And hit 73 home runs in a season! That also doesn't really count. What it does is keep him out of the Hall of Fame. McGuire at least admitted his transgressions. Bonds never has.

Need I remind you about Lance Armstrong, whose was stripped of his record-setting string of Tour de France victories for blood doping?

You might say that most elite athletes will do almost anything to get a leg up, to be **the best**. Sometimes, they don't get caught. Usually, they do. All because they weren't satisfied with being good. It's the gold medal that counts. Who remembers the runner-up? For example, can you name the last eight losers in the Presidential elections?

Theodore Roosevelt, himself a winner yet ultimately a loser, in his oft-quoted "man in the arena" speech, praises the man "who, if he wins, knows the triumph of high achievement; and who, if he fails, at least fails while daring greatly."

Yoga teaches us to do **the best** we can, and then to tell ourselves that "This is good enough." We learn that what is good today may be better or worse tomorrow. Yet it remains good enough. Being good enough just may be perfect for you. It is for me.

However, the joke still has merit. Even if it isn't **the best**.

Looking Good

I am all about looking. I notice things, perhaps more precisely than most. For a surgeon in practice for 32 years, that skill was imperative. I had selectively honed my visual skills to such a point that my ex-wife claimed I could spot a melanoma across a crowded room, while remaining quite capable of missing a bottle of Coke in the fridge.

It wasn't just the observational requirements of medicine that made me a good looker {Ladies, please do not misunderstand me; although the white coat can be flattering in an authoritative kind of way, that is not the subject at hand.}. These were my formative years in New York City, where there always has been far more than enough to arrest one's attention. A constant barrage of sights and sounds (other than during the eerie quietude of pandemics).

Let's limit ourselves to the former. There are, to name but a few: museums; window displays; kiosk advertisements; weird and wonderful new buildings and venerable classic structures; live performances on stage, in the ballparks, green spaces, and streets; altercations and criminal acts, often in broad daylight, occasionally before your very eyes; traffic snarls; and humanity. All ages, sizes, colors and attitudes. More than you can imagine unless you have been there to see for yourself.

I learned to look carefully early on—to look where I was going, lest I get run over or step in some poop, lest I trip on uneven pavement, lest I get mugged. I looked both ways before crossing, often against the light or in the middle of the street, as jaywalking in NYC is endemic and never prosecuted by the constabulary.

I looked up sometimes, trying to see the sky, a thing which is challenging amidst the plenitude of skyscrapers. I looked at the pretty girls who passed by—those who were chicly dressed and the ones in outrageous outfits. I looked at the graffiti, which exploded in my time from occasional to ubiquitous.

It was a veritable feast for the eyes, from Broadway shows and sporting events to the New York Public Library. I managed one trip to the top of the Empire State Building to look out in all directions over the vast expanse of city. The Statue of Liberty from close up presented an indelible vision.

Later on, I was trained to look for abnormalities in the human body, for sources of internal bleeding, for occult metastases on X-rays. I looked carefully to ascertain that each suture was correctly placed. I learned how to tell if a patient was being truthful or not from careful observation of their body language. I pored over miniscule details on patients' charts.

The art history classes and frequent museum trips I took helped sharpen my powers of observation. A number of medical schools of late are requiring art appreciation, along with the customary preclinical and clinical work, to enhance the critical skill of observation in those who have had more limited backgrounds. This will, in theory, contribute to making them better, more discerning physicians.

I thought I really knew something about how to look carefully, that is, until I became trained as a swim judge. Depending upon the level of competition, observation becomes more and more of a factor.

In judging little kids at a summer league event, where judges are hard to come by, one tends to spend most of one's time studiously looking the other way. Little infractions are glossed over, in the interest of not coming across as a nasty person who only wants to make kids cry and parents irate.

A championship meet is another story altogether. Normally, there are fifty-four judges at Nationals or in the Olympics! Three judges per lane at the start end, and one per lane at the turn end. Four judges are walking the sides of the pool. Four judges are standing in the corners, watching the other thirty-six judges, not the swimmers. There also are two relief judges. And a supervisory chief judge.

I won't bore you with the exact number of starters, deck refs, administrative refs, and meet refs. Just trust me when I say the number adds up to fifty-four. And every one of them is busy attending to whatever is in their purview.

That is one hell of a lot of looking. And I did this, for twelve years, often two weekends per month—while concentrating on surgery in my spare time. My eyes were bleary from all that looking.

I never rose to the exalted level of referee, let alone starter, at Nationals. But I reffed and started at plenty of meets on the local and regional level. I earned the soubriquet "Dr. DQ," not for overcalling infractions, but rather for having enough fortitude to make the appropriate call when the call needed to be made.

Watching swimmers is a challenging form of looking, especially since the judge has to look like he or she is not looking too hard, i.e., not looking for a reason to disqualify. No matter how egregious the swimmer's fault may be, any call may be overturned by an official higher up on the chain of command for any of the following reasons, among others:

1. The judge was not in proper position to see the infraction.
2. The judge delayed in raising their hand to indicate the disqualification.
3. There was confusion on the part of the judge in explaining the possible rule violation, such as not knowing which hand touched the wall first in cases where both must touch simultaneously.
4. The disqualification slip was incorrectly filled out.

All of which goes to show that what you see as you look may be disregarded. Yet, you better look like you are looking, or the ref will relieve you and find another judge who looks better.

I remember making one and only one disqualification call at Nationals. Standard protocol at this level is to take the judge who made such a call off the deck for a while— to recover from the stress. In my case, I felt no stress at all, compared with facing a belly full of blood and a rapidly falling blood pressure.

The referee asked me the standard questions. Subsequently, she scrutinized the DQ slip looking for errors. Finding none, the next question was, "Are you willing to talk to the coach?" Invariably the coach wants to protest the DQ and prefers to try to browbeat the judge rather than the ref, who has heard it all before and already is satisfied that the call was legitimate and properly supported.

In my case, there was no issue, because, after I notified the swimmer of my call, the swimmer said, "Yeah, I do that all the time. I usually don't get caught."

The ref, who isn't watching the swimmers, and may well not be watching the judges, needs to be aware of any unusual activity in the stands that could disrupt the proceedings. For instance, I was reffing a regional meet, when I noticed an agitated man waiving a gun way up at the top of the stands.

Being a surgeon, I am capable of fast decision making. I stopped the meet. I knew better than to confront the man. Instead, I called a coaches' meeting, pointed to the culprit (an irate parent who happened to be an off-duty security guard!), identified the appropriate coach, and told him to escort the man from the premises for the duration of the meet. Not until then did I allow the meet to proceed.

When you look for someone whom you have not seen for twenty-seven years, there is bound to be a certain amount of anxiety. Especially if that someone was the love of your life, until life got in the way of love and spoiled things. Also, because, after so many years, you are not at all sure whether you will be able to recognize her.

Over the phone we resolved to rendezvous at the steps of St. Patrick's Cathedral. At noon, in mid-November. Not a great decision, because St. Patrick's is on Fifth Avenue, and holiday shopping already was in full gear. Thousands were passing by in a mad crush. And plenty going into and out of the cathedral.

Here is where swim meet judging came in handy. A judge is taught to scan the lanes under their jurisdiction, not to focus on one swimmer more than the others. Scanning across three lanes is one thing; scanning a crowd is quite another. On this one day, I was looking all about.

At the Louvre, the *Mona Lisa* is perpetually surrounded by a railing and dozens of gawkers. Even if one patiently eases forward, one still cannot get within twenty feet of the painting. Yet, from any point in the room, once one engages her eyes, the crowd seemingly melts away. One sees at an emotional level that cannot be explained. This speaks to the genius of Leonardo.

On Fifth Avenue, at the steps of St. Patrick's, at noon, that mid-November day, two sets of eyes locked, instantly sweeping away decades of loneliness and teeming throngs of humanity.

And we two saw. We didn't just look. We really saw.

I Read, Therefore I Am

One's life is more formed, I sometimes think, by books than by human beings.
~ Graham Greene

Another pithy aphorism has it that one can tell a lot about a person by looking at their trash. Personally, I would prefer to see what's on their bookshelves. Less smelly.

If you define art as the creation of something to be observed, books—as they are appreciated in the design, either of text or cover—qualify. For that matter, so does music, considering live performance or study of the score, although not, strictly speaking, for appreciation of the sonorities.

What follows is an homage to the written word, which to me, in the hands of masters of the craft, is art.

I grew up and lived amidst books. My parents shelved them in our dining room and in the studio on the fourth floor of the family home in New York City. Not an overwhelming collection by any means, but the volumes were all hardbound, more than a few in leather. The covers were beautiful to look at and to feel. I remember doing just that, before any motivation to delve into the contents.

My parents were not voracious readers, although well-educated. They were physicians, science majors. *Compton's Encyclopedia*, as the final arbiter of all disagreements and the repository of almost everything we needed to know outside of medicine, was thumbed through more than anything else.

My own books soon overflowed a smallish bookcase plus the mantelpiece of my bedroom. Pretty soon, high school and college texts were spread here and there, space permitting, throughout the house. Not surprising for an English major, with a minor in music history. My pathway to medical school definitely was a departure from the norm.

My reading marked a progression from Landmark Books to Hans Christian Anderson, the Brothers Grimm, baseball history, *MAD Magazine*, Mark Twain, Edgar Allen Poe, and Robert Louis Stevenson. Thence to Shakespeare, Swift, Dickens, Hawthorne, and Hemingway. In college it was, among others: Greek tragedies; Chaucer, Shakespeare, and Milton; Enlightenment, Romantic, and Victorian poets and authors; Emerson, Thoreau, Whitman, Melville; Hemingway, Faulkner, and Fitzgerald.

After that, a frustratingly long break from literary classics for nine years of medical and surgical training. No more time for any reading but medical texts, surgical journals, and selected articles. All my beloved writers, of necessity, but not by choice, put aside. Mostly boxed up. But not forgotten.

Although my first apartment as a medical student and then as a surgical intern in New York afforded limited bookshelf space, my first house, in Bellevue, Washington, had more capacity. So, Dad shipped out a few boxes of my books. Not that there was much opportunity for a surgery resident, on call every other night. to read them. Yet it was a comfort having Dante, Ibsen, Goethe, and Homer close at hand, biding their time until we could have another go at it.

I took a job in Astoria, OR. We brought to a rented apartment a dog, zero kids, a microwave, and some pots and pans. Everything we owned fit into two cars and a U-Haul trailer. We borrowed a foldout bed and a Formica-top kitchen table from some friends who took pity on us. We transformed a wooden cable spool into a coffee table.

During those first four years following surgery training, while finally making decent wages, we began to replace those borrowed and found items with serious furniture, had two children, obtained a second dog, found a new home for the first one, bought a house, and filled up bookshelves. I discovered Dom De Lillo and read *Anna Karenina* and *War and Peace*, in between changing diapers, walking the dog, and performing operations.

Jumping at the opportunity to practice surgery in Seattle, we unhesitatingly gave the Astoria house back to its former owner. We returned with 21,000 pounds of household furnishings, which necessitated a large van and professional movers.

Freely admitting that Nature abhors a vacuum, we filled our new house with all manner of objects: paintings, sculptures, doll houses, not one but two elk heads, five desks, seven tables, four sofas, six file cabinets, a baby grand piano, and over twenty bookcases. Shelves galore! Room for my art and music history books. While settling in, I managed to find time to comprehend *Ulysses*, concurrently reading two explanatory books in order to have a better idea of what was going on.

Within five years there were four children, and we were into storage units for the overflow. At the peak of our excessive acquisitiveness, we had two garage-size and two half-size units, plus two storage pods outside the crammed-full garage, which, as could be expected, no longer afforded space for cars.

Although the house was way beyond cluttered, I managed to maintain a cozy, still-navigable den, complete with a padded wicker chaise lounge. I would put everyone to bed and snuggle in with *Don Quixote*, often falling asleep with the book in my lap, but ultimately getting all the way through. Incongruous as it may seem, reading Kafka facilitated the process of unwinding from typically hectic days.

I had become enthralled with all things related to Theodore Roosevelt and was starting to accumulate books by, about, or even only peripherally related to TR. And read almost all of them. My collection went far and wide afield to include vintage medical books and early editions of classic novels, short stories, biographies, plays, and poetry.

Most of my library accompanied me, when irremediable family matters required downsizing from an oversized four-bedroom house to an apartment. What with more book buying and the subsequent passage of fourteen years, I amassed well over 1,500 volumes.

In order to live full time in our smallish floating home on Seattle's Lake Union, we had to cull a quantity of books. My entire TR collection went to a university, as well as hundreds of tomes to the Seattle Library. Even with that, we needed to add considerable extra buoyancy to keep the place afloat. We made a number of contributions to the "little free libraries" that have popped up in various Seattle neighborhoods.

One of these was the depository for *Diamond Jim Brady: Prince of the Gilded Age*—a fun read about a real character, legendary for his personal diamond collection, as well as for his propensity for giving away hundreds more as gifts. Even better known for his super-sized appetite. {Google him, for sure.}

One day I got a call from Small Town, Florida. "Got this book here, Dr. Weber, that must have belonged to you. About Diamond Jim."

"Oh, yes, I recently read it and donated it to a neighborhood library. How did you get it?"

"Bought it on eBay. Always was fascinated with the man."

"Okay, but how did you link the book to me?" (My books are treated lovingly. No underlines or marginalia since college.)

"There's a voided check here with your name and address." (I must have used it as a bookmark.) "Do you want I should mail the check back to you?"

"No thanks, but please tear it up before you pass the book on, or sell it, to someone else."

I have managed to retain quite a few volumes at home. So many books and so little time. One would think, during this pandemic, that one would have ample time to read up a storm. My hero Theodore managed to read an average of more than a book a day. Even while serving as President! Even while exploring the course of an uncharted river through the Brazilian jungle.

The question is, why does it take me five weeks to read *The Education of Henry Adams*? You can say that we have more distractions these days: television, the internet, smart phones and watches. Our latest addition to the family, Louis, a rescued chihuahua-Italian greyhound mix, loves to walk. We let him lead us, often on four-mile jaunts. More than two hours of walking every day.

Then there are my daily Zoom yoga classes, bills to pay, emails to respond to, phone calls to return, household chores, shopping, daily meditation/naps, morning newspapers, evening news, food preparation, meals, and clean up, better sleep hygiene... I try to find time to write every day, not to mention tinkering with the (first) memoir that I started three years ago.

Now that I think of it, I am surprised that to be able to find time to read at all!

Mary reads the morning papers and *The New Yorker* religiously. Also an English major, she has read most of the standard classics. But she prefers not to reread books.

On the other hand, I enjoy rereading great works, which, sadly, in retrospect seem to have been underappreciated in school, when there was all that pressure to rush through them and move on. Now I feel qualified to bring to the rereading the requisite life experiences that make plot and characterization all the more vivid and transformative.

Books are pulled off the shelf that have sat, mostly unread, for half a century, assigned in college but only partly read. Mary was shocked to see me wading through

Thucydides' *History of the Peloponnesian Wars* at 3 a.m., thinking it hardly relevant to the teaching of yoga or to proper sleep habits.

What she didn't know was that after reading *Timon of Athens*, Shakespeare's treatment of Pericles had piqued my interest. I still had my Plutarch around, where his history was to be found. And Plutarch in turn inspired me to reach for Thucydides' fuller, more contemporary treatment. See how it goes with me?

No? Well try this. Prior to my first trip to Italy in over forty years, I thought it advisable to plow through Jacob Burkhardt's *The Civilization of the Renaissance in Italy*, also largely neglected, though assigned reading in college. Rick Steves' travel guides to Tuscany and Rome would have been easier reading and more pertinent, but I relished the opportunity to complete the assignment.

The first two times I read *Moby Dick* (in high school and again in college), for instance, I skimmed through, mostly skipping, the numerous chapters on cetology (the study of whales), since they did not seem to advance the plot, and I had to get on to *Billy Budd*. The third time, I read it the way Melville intended it to be read. Knowing full well how it was going to turn out did not detract from my enjoyment. The book morphed into an ebb and flow of the tides, as the compelling plot alternated with the biology of the huge marine mammals. It was a revelation.

Because reading does create a bit of a strain on the eyes, sometimes it is a relief to be read to. Robert Frost once wrote: "The ear, not the eye, is the best reader," which is especially true when considering the inherent music of poetry, with its rhythms and sounds. Prose also can evoke a certain rhythmic quality, as in Thomas Hardy's evocations of the moors at varying times of day and climatic conditions. Mary and I have enjoyed countless evening hours on our rooftop deck, lounging side by side in adjoining steamer chairs, hand in hand, being read to by a professional, often an actor. Always choosing the unabridged version.

Neither of us has had the slightest inclination to turn to Kindle. We spend enough time on our smart phones and laptops as is. There is something special about holding a book in your hands: the feel of it, the smell, the solitary experience. Reading is a kind of spiritual venture, an opportunity to tune out the auditory assaults of modern times and lose oneself in another world, another time.

A movie or television series adaptation of a book can capture some of the magic, but never all of the nuance. A reader's imagination can take him or her to deep emotional levels that a director cannot fathom. I have yet to watch a movie or TV version that seemed superior to the written word.

Let's say that you just selected a book to read, based upon a friend's recommendation, a review, or the memory of something started some time ago but never finished. How far should you go before deciding that you want to go no further, perhaps relegating it back to your shelves or giving it away? Sometimes you can tell from the first paragraph that this book is not for you, at least at this particular moment. Unless it happened to be written by your wife. Or by me. Just saying.

It can take a while to get used to an author's voice, style, or syntax. Reading Daniel Defoe is very different from James Clavell. Yet who is to say that *Robinson Crusoe* is less thrilling an adventure story than *Shōgun*? Expect something very different from Virgil than Mary Oliver. Both deserve your full attention, but that attention is yours to give, if and when you choose.

Are you of a mind to start a lengthy biography, like Ron Chernow's *Alexander Hamilton*? Maybe you want to verify the story behind the play. I love biographies, often keeping several on my night table at the same time. For instance, a few months ago, I was reading biographies of Haydn, Mozart, and Beethoven concurrently. All three were savored, yet all remain unfinished. That is my particular problem. I simply cannot bear to have any of the three die!

Short stories make for excellent bedtime reading, conducive to a restful sleep and pleasant dreams. Infinitely better than watching the evening news online or on TV. Try this: pick (almost) any letter of the alphabet, put your mind to it, and see if you can't come up with the name of an excellent short-story writer. Asimov, Baldwin, Chekhov... Go to the library and pick up one of their collections. You could make a game of it. You will have a problem coming up with an "X" author, other than Xenophon, but the *Anabasis*, although hardly a collection of short stories, won't disappoint, if you are interested in famous accounts of war.

Has all this reading has helped me become a better essayist? That is for you to determine. Just promise you won't compare my poor scribblings to the concepts, maxims, and conundrums of the greats. No need to reprove my efforts by thinking, *I knew Joan Didion, and you are no Joan Didion.* I know it, too.

VII. Fun and Games

Streaming Baseball

We are in our seats, midway along the third
base line, thirty rows up.

A group of eight of us shared four season seats. We met annually and drew lots to determine who got first dibs. I am not particularly lucky when it comes to chance, having never won anything more than a can of wallpaper paste, so I almost never got the Yankee games.

But that's okay because, growing up in New York City, I had frequent access to Yankee tickets. Even was there at The Stadium (which is what we all called it—just like NYC was always referred to as The City) with my Mom the day Don Larson hurled the only perfect game in World Series history. I had a miserable time of it because my Dodgers lost.

Here in Seattle, I almost always lost out on the primo picks. Generally, I got the leftover games, the Blue Jays, or the Twinkies, or whatever teams were mired—like my beloved Mariners, in the lean years that preceded the all-too-brief glory years (Don't get me started on the even leaner years that followed)—at or near the bottom of the standings.

But oh, those good years…

I was there in 1995 with my fourteen-year-old daughter, Katie, in the farthest corner of the very top row on the

300 level of the Kingdome, the day Edgar Martinez hit the double that drove in Griffey, Junior from first base and clinched the playoff series against those same dreaded Yankees. We were jumping up and down, cheering like there was no tomorrow. We were hugging total strangers. We were sobbing tears of joy, slobbering kisses all around as if we all were running for President, pre-pandemic.

Those were the Good Old Days, nothing like today, when you have to think twice and mask up, before stepping out of your house. This past year, baseball games were played in empty stadia, with cutouts in the seats and piped-in crowd noise. {Hope springs eternal; attendance restrictions for 2021 gradually are being lessened as of this writing.}

Ah, but back on that day of days, when we finished screaming and yelling, when our hands were raw from clapping, when the field was cleared of victory-lapping Mariners, when it was way past time for dinner, when we joined the 48,000-odd, ecstatic folks all exiting at once...

As we reached the street, Disaster reared her ugly head.

Did you know that I was a practicing surgeon? Well, I was, and I had my share of mishaps. Since then, I have gotten smarter and now teach yoga without having to worry about missing a referral if my cell phone was left on "Do Not Disturb" the whole day. I can watch baseball without interruption.

My brother lets nothing disturb him when he is

watching the Red Sox. He harbors a preternatural hatred of the Yankees. My dad grew up in Brooklyn, therefore, by definition, hating the Yankees. Only Mom, who knew almost nothing about baseball, professed to love them.

My wife Mary started out about as ignorant of baseball as Mom. I actually wrote a poem about this, from the depths of my frustration. It started with:

> We're talking baseball, my baby and I.
> She doesn't really know what I mean
> When I mention the infield fly rule,
> And the suicide squeeze sounds to her
> Suspiciously like the date from hell.

Back in 1995, cell phones were not smarter than we were. In fact, all they were good for was incoming and outgoing calls. Which is why doctors carried beepers (Think one-way text messaging). Which is why I panicked when mine went missing.

Have you ever been faced with going all the way back up to the top of a stadium from the street, in search of something left behind, while a sell-out crowd is in the process of exiting? You say you never had a beeper? You didn't miss much.

My brother unfortunately lost out on the only perfect World Series game in history. Don Larson vs. Sal "The Barber" Maglie (so called because he frequently threw his fastball high and tight, giving batters a close shave). I was there at that epochal game only because my brother preferred to go to watch Whitey Ford pitching the day before. He figured that would be more exciting. Ha-ha.

My daughter certainly was not amused when told that we would have to go back to try to find my beeper. Like salmon swimming against the current to spawn.

Which reminds me of the great Warren Spahn, pitching for a great Milwaukee Native American (my suggestion for a more PC name befitting this century) team. I was at Yankee Stadium during the 1957 World Series, as usual rooting against the Yanks. We were fortunate to have great complimentary seats.

> *So, we are sitting on the third base side for the umpteenth time, watching the woeful Mariners losing to another lousy team. Still, it's always fun to take the family to the ballpark.*

I digress here to tell you that despite having attended hundreds of ball games, I had never caught a foul ball. It wasn't simply that I was a lousy catcher. It was that balls never quite came to me, as I sat there, patiently waiting and breathlessly hoping. Without fail, they either would sail overhead or drop two rows away. I, of course, always had my mitt at the ready, just in case.

I could never play catcher in any games, being a leftie. It's a safe bet that you have never seen a left-handed catcher.

I bought Mary *The Complete Idiot's Guide to Baseball*,

written by the great, obviously right-handed catcher, Johnny Bench. I figured that she would not mind the not-so-subtle implication behind the title, since she had written several titles for the same outfit. Trying to teach her the cabalistic intricacies was, to quote again from my poem, "like teaching English as a second language to a Deaf-mute."

Mary has shown occasional willingness to absorb some of the myriad disconnected things I tell her (only on a need-to-know basis). Which is why I was hoping that she, especially having been an English major, might actually read the book. During the games.

Incidentally, Mary is not the only wife I ever had who was more or less disinterested in baseball. I seemed to attract the type.

By the way, that same year Don Larson did his thing, 1956, I got a rather unique type of Yankee team baseball. It featured stamped-on signatures, which was a lousy copout they did for a few years back then. "Signed" by Larry Berra, Ed Ford, (Who knew their real first names?) and everybody else from that legendary team.

It remained in its glassine wrapper for twenty-five years. Dad had kept it for me. He had it appraised for $1,500 in the early '80s.

Those of you who followed baseball in the early '90s probably remember Omar Vizquel, affectionately known as "Little O." You are more likely to think of him as a member of the Cleveland Indigenous Persons, but actually he was a

Mariner back then. And he would spray the whole section around me with comparatively worthless foul balls—every place but where I was sitting. I even actually stood up a few times a game, in hopes of a fortuitous carom. God forbid a focused laser beam should come directly at me.

Mary actually never got past the Fourth Inning (Chapter Four, get it?) of *The Complete Idiot's Guide to Baseball*. Her focus changed after three or four games to scanning the crowd, looking for her choice for "the baby of the game." She would narrow the field down to two or three little ones and then seek my opinion, typically during a critical moment, when the game was on the line, or when Omar was at bat. I would pick one of the kids randomly, without looking, whereupon she would begin to advocate for a different one. I would end up having to ask the guy next to me what just happened on the field.

What got her onto the babies was some wise-ass who watched her for a while and, no longer able to contain himself, blurted out something along the lines of "Don't you know that the game is down there? Why are you reading a book at a ball game?"

The second stanza of that same poem puts this into better context:

> Lots of fans go to watch the game;
> She watches the kids watching.
> Plus, she watches to see if I am
> Watching her to try to determine
> What exactly it is that she is watching.

Edie was also married to me. Not at the same time as Mary. She came along to the games with our older daughters, Emily and Katie. She was afraid that I might let them wander off in search of Dippin' Dots and lose their way. She kept one eye on each at all times, which was quite a trick, since they were sitting on opposite sides from her. She also brought reading material. And sometimes earphones.

Reading reminds me that there was another team baseball in the house, a 1947 Red Sox ball. Some of the signatures even were legible. And, yes, they were individually signed. Like team balls are supposed to be. Not like that stamped '56 Yankee ball. Jonny left it behind when he went off to college, and I used to play catch with it. Not often, mind you. Just when no other ball was handy.

But this has very little—okay, nothing—to do with Omar Vizquel, don't you agree? We can all agree that he was a terrific fielder and a respectable hitter.

Now, on the other hand, I was not a very good baseball player. You know how they say, "All hit, no field?" Well, I was pretty much no hit, no field. As a result, the '47 Red Sox ball would get dropped now and then. And scuffed on the sidewalks. Or stained a bit with the neatsfoot oil that we all used to deepen and soften the pockets of our mitts, and to help us feel, or at least smell, more like real baseball players. Ted Williams' name was one of the few that still could be identified. Likely thanks to the kind intervention of the baseball gods.

I thought it especially decent of the cleanup crew that they started cleaning the area around the slightly less cheap seats first. Thank God, I found my beeper—when Katie and I bucked the flow of the exiting masses to where we had been sitting—in the "Bob Uecker seats" {worthwhile to Google, even if you get my meaning in context}. There it was, lying right in the middle of a scattering of peanut shells, hot dog roll shards, and beer. And still working. Smelling like a baseball stadium.

> *The particular game I keep trying to tell you about happens to be on "Family Night." It is also Stevens Hospital Night, which means that many of those who work with me are there at the ballpark.*

Stevens Hospital had a summer softball league, and I played in it. It was a "Jack and Jill" league, which meant that there were more than a few women out there who could hit the ball farther than I. There always seemed to be a few gals who looked good holding a bat, but were automatic outs. I didn't look as good, yet the opposing pitchers, possibly feeling sorry for me, would occasionally manage to hit my bat with the pitch, occasionally resulting in a squibbler or a blooper that got me safely to first base.

My brother had worked with my swing, for what it was worth, in the upstairs studio of our house in NYC.

We would wad up newspapers as bats and try to throw tricky pitches with our Whiffle Ball. I tried to apply what he taught me to our HS stickball games.

In the Stevens Hospital softball league, where real bats were used in place of broomsticks, the men had to bat wrong-handed. This for me was not such a challenge, since I was a mediocre hitter at best batting on my "good" side. I think I ended up slightly better batting on my "bad" side than I ever was before—not saying much.

> *So...Family Night and Stevens Hospital night. Half of our softball league must be here, watching "Little O" foul off pitch after pitch. You probably can guess where I am going with this, but I will describe it in excruciating detail anyway. Omar slices a fly ball. It is coming right towards me. OMG.*

I did try to catch a foul ball some years later in the seats behind the plate. The thing went up for what seemed like miles. This was late in a game that didn't matter, and everyone had left the ballpark, except those who were paid to stay. Including the wives. It was September, and it was cold. For once, I didn't bring my glove.

I almost lost sight of the ball as it soared into the Empyrean. Then the ball came down, like a ton of bricks. And I am an idiot for trying to catch it. Of course, I couldn't haul it in. The only other fan still remaining in the stadium circled behind me and scarfed it up on the rebound.

At least, I still retained the '47 Red Sox ball, although it really belonged to my brother. As I said, he is, and ever shall be, world without end, a Red Sox fan. Except when they have a losing record. Jonny was so hooked that he seriously contemplated chucking it all (which wasn't much, as he was about to retire anyway) and following the team around for a whole year. He wrote his friend Dennis Eckersley that he planned to chronicle his travels with the Sox. When it was pointed out that Stephen King had already done that, Jonny stayed with his day job.

I had a boarding school and college roommate named Steve Greenberg, who also passed up a chance to travel all over the country on behalf of baseball, in this case, as commissioner. He opted to keep his day job, too, at a law firm in NYC.

In one of our stickball games, Greenberg once hit a ball so far that we had to go get another ball. No wonder. His father was a Hall of Famer.

Personally, I never got much wood on the ball in stickball, but I was a crafty pitcher, although not crafty enough to throw a ball past Greenberg. I used all those spins Jonny taught me with the Whiffle Ball.

> *Omar's foul ball is spinning my way. Holy Cow. I stand up, a bit weak in the knees, glove at the ready.*

I since have lost my beloved baseball glove and feel disinclined to replace it, considering that I am seventy-three and have nobody around to play catch with. And no business playing catch at my age, either.

Ushers, almost all up there in age, get lots of balls hit into the stands during batting practice. I suppose they give most of them away to kids. Maybe they have to do that as a condition of their employment. Getting a ball is a real thrill for anybody, at any age, any way it comes to you.

Catching a bag of roasted peanuts is fun, too. The Mariners have a guy who is awesomely accurate throwing bags of roasted peanuts, always behind his back. He wins contests of roasted peanut bag throwing. They really have such things. Rick the Peanut Man is legendary around Seattle. He can whip those bags at you from forty feet with amazing accuracy. He never misses. He is practically perfect.

You can take the qualifier out when you talk about that particular World Series game. I was all of eight and knew enough about the game to know that it was depressing that no single Dodger player could find his way to first base. For any reason. And I, a precocious Dodger fan, winced in my seat next to my mother who was all "Lah-di-dah; the Yanks win again" and "Nah, nah; your Dodgers are terrible." Rubbing it in. My own mother. Putting me on the defensive.

The Vizquel ball is finding its way towards me with frightening accuracy. Not having sufficient time to duck, I put my glove up in self-defense, not to mention trying to protect the family.

Offence and defense are radically scaled down in stoopball. You take one of those hollow pink balls that were ubiquitous in the '50s and '60s. You bounce it on the pavement so that it rebounds off the stoop. Then you watch it rebound up into the air and try to gauge how far it will travel. Rules are made up on the fly.

Usually, there is at least one other kid in the game, because it really isn't much fun playing stoopball by yourself. I tried that once in my bedroom, and, when the pink ball arced upwards, I leaped up from my bed and tried to catch it, evoking Willie Mays, kind of, managing to fall backwards off the bed and see stars for the first time in my life.

Katie has two balls signed by stars: one signed by both Griffeys; the other by Edgar Martinez. I hope she still has them anyway. Emily has one signed by Harold Reynolds.

Mickey Mantle certainly was a star. He had his knee repaired more than once by Sid Gaynor, a family friend, and, like most of us in the family, a physician. Each year the Yankees made it to the Series, Sid Gaynor would get bunches of tickets. Dutifully, he would give my family two tickets to two games. Growing up in the '50s and '60s and having an arrangement like that was perfect for me.

You can look up all the years that the Yankees were in the World Series and usually won, to my chagrin. I was at quite a few of those games.

The Red Sox, on the other hand, had a nearly 100-year span of not winning the World Series. Until 2004. Jonny was so excited about their chances of actually winning that he wrote his buddy Eckersley and managed to obtain two tickets to all the games. That should have meant one for me. After all, we are brothers, aren't we? We were always close enough.

I recall plenty of close encounters with another avid Red Sox fan. This was Bart Giamatti. He was a Renaissance literature scholar, and Greenberg and I took a semester course from him at Yale. Giamatti gave up the presidency of Yale University to become president of the National League and then commissioner of baseball. He didn't last long.

It hardly takes any time for Vizquel's foul ball to reach me.

Nor did Mary's attention to the events on the ball field last for more than an inning or two. Looking at babies was more interesting to her. Not that we ever had any. We started too late.

I had a girlfriend in 1967 who preferred to go to see the movie *Hawaii*, instead of watching the one-game playoff between the Red Sox and the Twinkies. She obviously needed to have her priorities adjusted. Undaunted, I took my transistor radio and earphones and listened to the game, which was memorable. Don't ask me about the movie. The important thing was that the BoSox won the game.

I was hoping to be remembered as something more than a surgeon. Perhaps a second career. Ushering at M's games had great appeal, but ushering doesn't help much with household bills. Neither does teaching yoga, come to think of it. Catching and subsequently selling a prized baseball, even if you risked your life to get it, pays better. Even if it didn't take any effort, and, for instance, a record-breaking Bonds home run ball magically dropped onto your hot dog.

> *Wouldn't you know it? I catch that Vizquel ball! Or rather, it catches me. Call it destiny. Emily, Katie and I are ecstatic. Everyone in the stadium is treated to a video replay on the giant Diamond Vision screen, because, after all, it is Family Night. I am relishing my three seconds of fame.*

I ended that baseball poem, for which I expect never to be famous, with a fervent hope that my few readers will cherish the inherent value of the game. I was channeling my inner Giamatti, paraphrasing a concept from his book, *Take Time for Paradise*:

When we talk baseball, we talk about life
And goals and deeply felt desires.
What for instance could be more basic
Than the concept of winning the game
By coming home successfully?

Baby Betsy is five and at home in the time of Omar Vizquel and the Legendary Foul Ball. She already has learned to channel surf on the TV. Likely looking for Smurfs, she instead finds Daddy holding up a ball and her big sisters jumping up and down for joy. She hollers (which she excels at) to the babysitter to "Come see Mommy and Daddy and Emily and Katie on TV!"

Giamatti was on TV a lot during the fracas over Pete Rose, who was caught betting on the outcome of games while managing the Cincinnati franchise. Giamatti had kept the Yale connection to Major League Baseball going by bringing in his buddy Fay Vincent to be assistant commissioner. A few weeks after banning Pete Rose from baseball for life, Giamatti departed his. Fay Vincent, now commissioner, felt obliged to bring in another Yalie— none other than my old friend, roomie, and fellow English major Steve Greenberg—to be his assistant. And so it goes.

At Yale, my English senior year project was to read everything Herman Melville ever wrote. In fact, I have read *Moby Dick* three times. Edie knew that. All my wives have known that. It could be my main claim to fame. I cannot help but see in the Mariners' hitherto hopeless quest to get to the World Series a similarity to that of Ahab (himself a mariner) chasing the Great White Whale.

Hospital personnel keep coming up after the fact and telling me that they saw me triumphantly holding aloft that little white ball. They laugh about the kids jumping up and down with joy, the evident look both of shock and exhilaration on my face. They remark that Edie, right beside me, showed no emotion at all. That it's too bad she missed the chance to smile on TV.

Actually, Rick the Peanut Man flipped a few of his patented behind-the-back bag tosses toward me, and I caught all but one. The one I missed might not have been my fault, as it ended up two rows back and two seats over from me. Hit an unsuspecting old guy upside his head and splattered peanuts like rain throughout our section. Rick certainly felt bad. The old guy was pretty sore.

And I got to feeling worse and worse about hanging onto that Red Sox ball. After all, I had a few others. I had retained it for over forty years, and enough was enough. The Red Sox finally won a World Series, so the time seemed right to tell Jonny that I had a present for him.

For years, Jonny had me believing that the Red Sox never lost a game. He told me that sometimes they would be vying for low score, other times for high score. The determination as to the object of any particular game was never made until after the game was over. He was my big brother. Why would I doubt anything he said? I held on to that belief longer than the reality of Santa Claus.

I held on to a position on the board of the Seattle Symphony for nearly six years. The big draw for me was that the Mariner team president's wife was also on the board. I got her to ask her husband, Chuck Armstrong, for a few favors along the way. Hence the Griffey ball for Katie, plus the opportunity to sit in the dugout with Edgar Martinez on her birthday (and get a signed ball). Also, a Fourth of July photo with Harold Reynolds at home plate on Emily's birthday (with another signed ball.). And I handed over my prize ball to have "Little O" sign it, right before he shipped out to Cleveland.

A neighbor calls me up the day after my Vizquel heroics to tell me that he recorded the whole game and figures that I deserve the tape. I only have a Betamax, but I accept the VCR tape graciously all the same.

Jonny accepted the '47 Red Sox ball tearfully after saying grace at our Thanksgiving dinner. Although it was yellow with age, he appeared not to mind the damage done by my repeatedly dropping it on the street while playing catch. The scuffs were way beyond repair, yet he seemed glad enough to make out the signatures of Ted Williams and one or two others.

I am despairing that Mary will never wade all the

way through nine innings of Johnny Bench's signature literary effort, although she now more or less can explain the suicide squeeze without raising her heart rate. This is much further than any previous wives or girlfriends have gotten in their appreciation of the game.

> *For example, as the ball strikes my open mitt and actually stays there, Edie is immersed in* Moby Dick. *On tape. With headphones. Sitting right next to me. As I catch a foul ball. AND NOT EVEN NOTICING.*

One cannot help but be aware that the value of an Omar Vizquel-signed baseball will go up if Little O ever makes it into the Hall of Fame. Some say he will, others say he won't quite make it, having failed, through no fault of his own, to achieve the stature of other great shortstops. In any case, he will be on the ballot for a few more years.

That should give me time to find a used VCR machine. First, I suppose I should try to find the tape. I'm sure it is stashed away in some safe place.

As for the ball, God only knows what has happened to it. "Easy come, easy go," as they say.

'Nuff said.

Thar's Gold in Them Thar Roses

In ballet or modern dance, a performer can, and often does, execute a fall with perfect grace. This requires considerable athleticism and body control. My former friend Tex, neither a dancer nor an athlete, once pulled off something similar. He was walking around the dinner table, pouring red wine, lost his balance and managed to keel over, without spilling so much as a drop. It was the epitome of ad hoc choreography. He fell silently onto the rug, rolled over, bounced back up, and resumed pouring.

Tex is pretty short, so I suspect I might have been the only one who actually noticed that he had fallen.

The only other times I saw anything remotely like this were: (a) when Mary, herself a former dancer, accomplished a freeze-frame fall into the lake, the first and only time she attempted to get into our canoe; and (b) when she swung her leg over her brand-new bike and forgot to stop at the seat. Please do not get me wrong— these performances were slow-motion marvels. It is possible to be simultaneously clutzy and lissome, at least for the chosen few.

Tex had another claim to fame. He grew prize-winning roses. Quickly outgrew the confines of his front and back yards. Expanded onto the neighbors' property on both sides of the street. Took some of his blossoms to rose shows and won prizes. Began a rose-garden-caretaking business. Actually gave up his day job.

One of the gardens where Tex was wont to work his magic happened to belong to none other than the wife of Trader Bob. Here was a man who had zero interest in roses, except perhaps on Valentine's Day. He stepped out on his back porch one fine evening.

"That's a nice job you are doing with the wife's flowers," or something to that effect. I wasn't there, so I am imagining how it went.

"Well, thanks."

Not quite the end of the conversation. Trader Bob, per usual, is contemplating another player move. After all, he is, or was at different times (sometimes at the same time), the general manager of the Seattle Seahawks and the late, lamented SuperSonics, as well as the Portland Trail Blazers.

Some might prefer to sit on the porch, watch the sunset, and zone out. Or watch the gardener for a spell. Trader Bob was always fixated on trades, 24/7. Some big, some small, some blockbusters. Some successful. Too many less so. Which is why he no longer is a general manager.

"Say, Bob, do you mind if I ask you something?" Thus was the reverie of a potentially beautiful deal interrupted. "Is there some reason why my seats at Seahawks games haven't improved, even after ten years as a season ticket holder?" A leading question, if I ever heard one. Even if I didn't actually hear it.

"Let me see what can be done."

The rose bushes must have been really nice, because, four days later, Tex received two seats on the fifty-yard line, fourteen rows above the playing field, where Trader Bob occasionally is to be found, assessing potential trade bait.

Now, Tex may be vertically challenged, but he is not reticent. And why would he be, after winning prizes at flower shows?

"Thanks for the seats. Can I have two more?" Just like that.

And, sure enough, he got them!

Not for free; but by selling two seats per game to ticket agents, he easily paid for all four. And had enough money left over to buy dim sum at the International District on his way to the games.

He invited me to a game. I had given up my season tickets a few years before, as Seahawks games were hardly fun family events. It seemed like the game, for almost everyone sitting around us, was merely an excuse for drinking vast quantities of beer. As if that's not bad enough, add to it having beer spilled on us virtually every game by overly-exuberant fans standing up to signal touchdown, forgetting the drink in their hand. Might I add that the noise was deafening. My ears would be ringing for 45 minutes after each game.

Still, I knew Tex's seats were primo, so I took him up on the offer. The dim sum was on me. We stopped at a convenience store for a soda, which in those days you could sneak into the stadium. Nobody was checking for knives, guns, bombs, or much of anything else. I picked out a Coke.

"What do you want, Tex?"

"I dunno." The repercussions of the "dunno" went on for upwards of five minutes. There might have been a dozen soft drinks from which to choose.

For example: "What about a Dr. Pepper?"

"I dunno. Maybe."

Or, "There's a nice cold 7 Up here. Want that?"

"Maybe. Let me think about it." *Are you kidding? What is there to think about?*

"Oh look. They have Dad's Root Beer."

"That may be good." *Jesus tonight, it **is** good. Good enough.*

"You know, I'm just not sure…" *How sure do you need to be?*

"I have an idea. I will think either of the number one, or the number two. If you guess the number I am thinking of, I will pick out a soft drink for you. If you guess the wrong number, I will buy you a bottle of water."

"Sparkling or flat?" *Yay. We are making progress!*

But then: "You know, I don't really like playing games like this. I always lose."

"Okay. Suppose I select five soft drinks, assign each a number, and have you pick a number between one and five. That way you can't lose."

"Yeah, but I might get a drink I don't like."

"Well then you can have my Coke. I will drink any of these."

"I only drink Diet Coke."

"Perfect. They have that right here."

"Yeah, but I'm not in the mood for Diet Coke." I am in the mood to punch him in the face. The last time I actually followed through on such an impulse—really the only time—was in high school.

"Tell you what. I'll give you your ticket, and you go ahead. I'll make my choice and meet you at the game." Surprising turn of events, but *Hallelujah*, nonetheless.

I am in my seat, straddling the midfield stripe, fourteen rows above the floor as promised. Brent Musburger is sitting right behind me. That's how good these seats are. Sports broadcasting royalty though he is, he is drinking a Coke, just like me. Tex shows up halfway through the first quarter.

"So, which soda pop did you choose?"

"None of them. I couldn't make up my mind."

"Tell you what, I'll spring for a beer during the half."

"No thanks, but I will take a Diet Coke, if they have it."

"Why didn't you just let me buy you one at the convenience store?"

"I didn't think I would want one then."

Tex and his wife actually made the decision to remodel their lovely home on Mercer Island. I was over there before they had the work done, the time when Tex had done his spotless half somersault.

I also saw the place after the renovation. I thought it looked great. But then I thought it was great before the overhaul. I knew better than to say that.

"Wow, you two really have this place looking fabulous."

"Do you think so? I'm kind of sorry we changed things around. We should have thought more about it before having all this work done. Now we are talking about restoring the place to its original floor plan. I'm just not sure."

Tex called me up about going to another game a year or so later. I made a quick decision and declined. Haven't heard from the man since.

No Joke

For those of you who are thinking about a career as a health club instructor, here's the stipulation: You must teach two or more classes a week for LA Fitness, in order to maintain a complimentary pass, valid at any of their clubs. Why anyone would want to be working out in gyms in this time of COVID-19 is another matter.

I taught for ten years or so at LA Fitness. I had heard they were opening a new facility and called the regional fitness director to offer my services as a certified yoga teacher. As soon as she told me her name was Chrissie Krystl, I knew this would be a good fit. I always have adored alliteration. She gave me a tryout.

"We can pay you eighteen dollars an hour." This is a bit of a comedown for a general surgeon.

"I won't teach yoga for less than thirty-five. You may not know this, but I am a doctor, also certified as an Ayurvedic Counselor."

She didn't know what Ayurveda is. In case you do not know either, Ayurveda is Indian natural medicine. About as different from Western medicine as Neanderthals are to *Homo sapiens.*

The field encompasses, through a wealth of accumulated experience and the wisdom of the ages: the use of herbs; daily cleansing rituals; non-FDA approved, often home-cooked medications; astrology; gemology; meditation; and, yes, yoga.

Chrissie Krystl was subjected to a quick précis of Ayurveda and an earful about integrating western medicine, Ayurveda, and yoga into my teaching. Her eyes began rolling with all this information. Browbeaten into agreeing to my requested wages.

Predictably, I never received any cost of living raises after that. But then, nobody ever did at LA Fitness, so far as I know. Not the instructors, nor the desk attendants, nor the janitors, nor the sales force. Nor any of the club managers, which may be why we went through seven of them during the time I worked there.

I wasn't doing this work for the money. I enjoyed my students, loved teaching yoga enough to give up my surgery practice, and had no objection to being paid, however little, to stay fit.

I taught half of my twelve weekly classes at LA Fitness, becoming somewhat of a rock star. Not to boast, but, as Dizzy Dean once said, "It ain't bragging if you can back it up." My students would pack up their mats and walk out, if another teacher showed up in my place. They only retained their membership so they could continue to take my classes.

That was because I made yoga fun. While persistently encouraging diligence, I tried to keep things light with some nonessential banter or anecdote. Occasionally, I threw in a history quiz.

The "yoga studio" was nothing of the sort. It was yoga in a multi-use gym. Worse, there often was a spinning class next door. The walls were thin, and the cycling enthusiasts, being for the most part masochists, always insisted that the instructors bellow or scream at them. Music during yoga was a must to help muffle the noise from next door.

I usually opted for classical selections, with special playlists for holidays, and occasional jazz or ragtime pieces thrown in for variety. Two students offered to perform live music for my classes, synced to my teaching. The students loved it.

Administration was not so sure. They expected us to play only LA Fitness-approved yoga music (which none of the teachers ever did). What convinced them to look the other way were the salesmen who used to promote club membership by saying, "And we even feature live music in yoga class!"

One of my students called what I was doing "Yoga, plus." I love this.

The front desk reception job was a revolving door. Rarely would anyone, for minimum wages, stay for more than a year. Regardless, they soon got to know who I was, because students would call and ask, "Is James teaching today?" (LA Fitness insisted on calling me James because that was the name on my paycheck. Hitherto, I had only been called James when my wife was vexed at me.)

I never used my fob to check in—instead, nodding to

the desk and walking through. If challenged at the desk by a newcomer, I would simply say that I was the yoga teacher.

This always worked. Well, almost always.

On one particular day, my usual attempt to breeze through was rejected.

"Excuse me. You need to check in." This from a twenty-something-year-old woman, likely unhappy that this scofflaw was interrupting her texting.

"No need. I am the yoga teacher."

She put down her cell phone, scrutinized me, gray-haired, wizened and all, and blurted out, "You're kidding!"

Rejected and rebuked. Rendered speechless. Dumbfounded. Blindsided by a Gen Z'er. It was like the first time somebody offered me their seat on the bus. It was worse than the day I turned fifty and got my first letter from AARP.

Saved by one of my faithful students, explaining, "It's okay; he really is our yoga teacher," I went and did my thing.

Five years later, I am still at it, although not yet fortified with an appropriate retort, should this kind of thing come up again {Not likely while teaching yoga by Zoom—my gig for the past year.}.

Any ideas?

Brownie Points

I really did get lucky in reconnecting with Mary, half a lifetime after we had first met. My situation was somewhere between a mess and a disaster. The practice of surgery was becoming oppressive, analogous to the albatross around the neck of the Ancient Mariner in Coleridge's poem. My health was precarious at best, eating habits erratic, and sleep near bottom on the satisfaction scale.

Mary took a look at this trainwreck of a man and, from the very first opportunity, started a rehabilitation project that continues to this very day.

Now, sixteen years later, I freely acknowledge that I would not be teaching yoga or writing, let alone breathing, were it not for her. I must be giving her some return for her loving efforts, as she has told me that I "make God real {for her}."

I once asked her what I could do to be a better husband, and she said, "All you have to do is breathe."

I thought, *I should do more than that,* so I put my mind to coming up with a special present for her birthday. Annually, I had been asking for a hint, yet, all I ever got was, "I have everything I ever wanted." While one couldn't hope for a clearer expression of gratitude, a bit more direction might have been nice.

I always answered my four daughters specifically when they asked me: "What can we get you for your birthday, Daddy?"

"A urinal." Unless you have lived in a house with four daughters and their mother, you would not understand.

Anyway, I never got one, until being hospitalized with my first heart attack. If and when you get released, you get your clothes back, plus any of the freebies you want to pile into a bag. Like the cheap toothbrush, comb, Kleenex box, slipper-socks, plastic water pitcher...

"What do you want with that urinal?"

"Please, nurse, can't I have it?"

"No, not that metal one. I guess you can take one of these disposable ones, if you really want." Of course, I wanted. The kids had never taken my request seriously. It was my only chance.

Anyway, that was then. This is also then, but more recently. And I have come up with an idea.

Mary and I first met at a Yale Alley Cat concert at her Alma Mater. I had three solos, "Five Foot Two," "They Can't Take That Away from Me," and "All My Trials." Nearly five decades later, she occasionally tormented me with pleas for a repeat performance. Almost always during the two-minute drill of a particularly, or should I say typically, down-to-the wire Seahawks game.

"Tell you what—I will sing the former if we win. It's about the height of Russell Wilson. Either of the other ones I suppose would work if we lose."

Somehow, I never got around to performing any of them. Which was just as well, as the old pipes were a bit rusty.

The last thing I had sung outside of the shower was "America the Beautiful" at the end of yoga class on Independence Day. I had a lot of help, as the whole class joined in. Instead of "OM," we launched right into "O beautiful for spacious skies..."

This spontaneous outpouring of patriotic strains in the yoga studio put a notion into my head...

Teaching yoga breathwork is inspiring.

One of my better ideas, aside from the literary light bulbs that continue to pop into my head during class, concerned Valentine's Day. Mary was scheduled to teach water aerobics.

"Do you want me to get a sub for next Tuesday, honey?"

"Why would you do that?"

"Well, it is Valentine's Day..."

"Oh gosh, I forgot." (Subterfuge. I had a secret plan in the works.) "And I am scheduled to teach yoga that morning, too. I guess we might as well go do our classes. We can have a nice, quiet celebratory afternoon after that. For one thing, hopefully we will be able to celebrate not receiving another Valentine's Day subpoena from my ex-wife."

Here is what actually did happen: I went one direction to teach yoga, while Mary went elsewhere for her water aerobics class. I ended my class a few minutes early so that I could haul ass to where Mary was teaching. I got there just in the nick of time to see the barbershop quartet I had hired march onto the pool deck in semi-formal attire to serenade Mary in front of forty-five loyal class attendees who stood there in amazement and clapped at the end, hoping for an encore. And then exited the pool, dripping wet, to hug me.

I got more attaboys for that caper than for guaranteeing Biden's victory the morning after Election Day, which I did because I am not afraid to go out on a limb and am often inordinately optimistic. Water aerobics participants continued to ask me for years afterwards what I was planning for the following Valentine's Day. Clearly, they wanted to know how I could top that one.

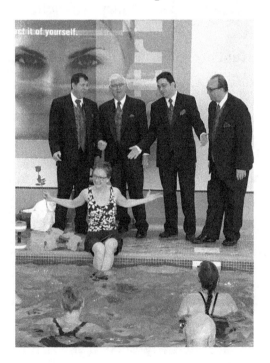

I couldn't. Not until the particular birthday I am getting to—and the notion.

Previously, I mentioned having two talented instrumentalists in my class. They often would show up unannounced with cello and guitar in their respective hands and synchronize some lovely tunes to my asana instruction.

"Would you two help me out with a little project?" I was thinking that it would be hard for them to refuse me, since playing music for my classes was where they got the confidence to put together a combo to play at bars, neighborhood block parties, and even a wedding or two.

"I want to record a couple of songs as a present for Mary."

Eyes lit up, as they were contemplating a paid gig. That wasn't part of the plan. Anyway, they said yes. I listed the songs, which fortunately they were old enough to recognize. We found half an hour to practice surreptitiously in the apartment, while Mary was getting her hair cut.

"I think 'Five Foot Two' would sound better with a ukulele." *Hmm—ukulele and cello. Why not?*

"Bring it with you when we find another time slot, this time to record—of course, on the sly."

On the appointed day, a member of the Seattle Opera Chorus happened to be in yoga class. Not one to look a gift horse in the mouth, I asked, "Gail, would you happen to be free this afternoon at 3 p.m. to record a few duets with me?" What could she say?

Okay, she could have said no, wise guy. But she didn't.

We got some decent takes on the second try.

On the morning of Mary's birthday, I excused myself from her excellent company and repaired to the desktop computer in the living room.

"Hey! What do you think you are doing? It's my birthday, and, at the very least, I deserve a hug."

"Just a minute, honey."

"...What are you doing?"

"Just checking my email." I suspect that she is contemplating taking back all those wonderful things she said to me about God and breathing. Hungarians are known for their tempers. Even though she is only half Hungarian, you don't want to get her riled up.

"Would you mind coming in here? You can collect three hugs if you want."

And she got her birthday present: three musical hugs. Recorded for posterity.

Fade to Black

For over a year now, I have been teaching yoga exclusively by Zoom. Six days a week. It definitely has taken a while to get adjusted to the new reality. Not so much, the technical mechanics or the spatial limitations. Those murky waters were easy enough to navigate.

More challenging was the frequency with which the students and/or their pets would come and go, leaving in their wake an empty screen, or flipping their video image off and on. Some could be seen picking up their cell phones and talking or texting, as if being muted to the rest made this acceptable. Much as I love animals— and my loyal students, for that matter—I found all of this somewhat distracting, especially at first.

On the other hand, there are some terrific perks to teaching by Zoom: notably, no travel time or expense. Depending upon the starting time, I literally can roll out of bed or finish up any number of chores before teaching a class. I confess to being prone not infrequently to cutting it close. This seems to be okay with the students, who are lonely from their prolonged pandemic isolation and more than happy to chat a bit before class actually starts.

Joining at the eleventh hour, sometimes I feel like I shouldn't short-circuit the socializing. But that's not what I get the big bucks for, so I take a stand, or more likely a cross-legged seat, and give them fair warning that they are about to be muted. Hitting the "Mute All" is a real power move.

I prefer to keep things light. My job, as I see it, is 60% teaching yoga, 30% cheerleading and encouraging. The other 10% of the time, I tell stories and/or recommend TV series, specials, movies, and books. Yoga, plus. Right?

For instance, just before starting class the other day, I told my students the following about a nearby hummingbird nest:

> "The nest is four doors down the dock from us, perched on a string of leftover Christmas lights under the eaves of the entry to another floating home. Made in part from spider silk and perhaps two inches maximum in diameter, it is hardly larger than the light bulbs."

One by one, my students started sharing their own experiences with hummingbird nests—emphasizing how precarious the whole birthing, growth, and development situation can be for this species. We were well past the starting time, but I had more to tell. It had to wait. I muted all and initiated the class with the usual grounding, yogic breathing, centering, and 3 OMs. Then, and only then, as we started going through our warm-up stretches, I did I go on with the story:

"I am worried and have been walking down the dock with Louis several times a day to check on the nest, where the prospective mama sits all day and, presumably, all night."

One of my students unmuted herself to tell the rest of us significant factoids about exactly how much a hummingbird needs to eat to stay alive. A few more students unmuted to add items of interest—that these birds cannot walk or hop, are uniquely able to fly backwards, have outsized brains, etc. So much unmuting, with everyone talking at once, that we soon had a situation of incipient chaos, which was distinctly counterproductive to yoga, and unsettling to me.

In desperation, I cut them all off. *After all*, I thought, *who is in charge here anyway?* I got them back on the right track and put them through another ten minutes of warmups before continuing the subject at hand:

"When Louis and I walked by again today, the bird was nowhere to be found. Two possibilities came to mind. One was that Starlings or crows had raided the nest in search of a little *amuse-bouche* {or beak}. The other was that Mini-mama had flown off in search of nourishment. Moments later, she was zigzagging around us, stopping in mid-air a foot away to scrutinize me and then dropping down to Louis' level to check him out. {No obvious stink eye, but then it would be hard to tell with a hummingbird, wouldn't it?} Then she zipped back to the nest."

End of story, as we moved on to Vedic Sun Salutations, which are simple to perform when taught correctly, but a bit tricky to teach in terms of keeping the movements carefully synced to the breath. I almost always do these sun salutations with my eyes closed, so that I really can be in tune with the flow and not be distracted by extraneous student activities.

I went through the six sequences, teaching every step carefully, humming right along {You knew that was coming, didn't you?}, and then opened my eyes to find the screen dark. The laptop had powered off!

In my zeal to tell my wife about the close encounter with Mini-mama and in the rush to set up my yoga space, I had forgotten to connect my laptop to the charger. I always try to remember to plug it in, because battery power often is down after writing stories such as this late into the night.

This has happened a few times now. It takes two uncomfortably long minutes for the laptop to power on again. The students are more or less okay with this little break, often unmuting and chatting until I get back on.

I came back online and asked whether they all finished the sun salutations, assuming that the computer quietly turned itself off part-way through. Several looked a bit puzzled, but one gave me a thumbs-up and nodded his head in assent.

It turned out that the power had not been off for a few seconds plus the two minutes to recharge. It had been off for well over ten minutes, while I blithely, blissfully, and blindly taught sun salutations to nobody.

The one student who indicated that they had finished the sun salutations without me was fibbing, because they never saw me exhorting them to start. Instead, they talked some more about hummingbirds, speculated a bit about what might have happened to me, and then decided that they would take turns leading the class, trying to recreate my normal set of directions.

This inveterate dissembler had grown up in Ireland, in Belfast no less, where one needs at times to be willing to stretch the truth in order to stay alive.

That said, I cannot tell a lie. It was distinctly uncomfortable to realize just how long I been left in the dark.

Which may—or may not—prove my point: *You never know.*

Acknowledgments

First and foremost, I credit Bob James, the famous jazz pianist and producer, whom I have never met and likely never will. He provided a blueprint for me. *Rameau*, his fabulous album of synthesized Baroque music has been one of my favorites since its release in 1984. But, more than the wonderful collection of tunes, the way in which it all came together has resonated with me ever since I read the liner notes. James created these pieces as Christmas presents for friends and ultimately acquiesced to their suggestion that he assemble them into a whole album.

In a similar way, I wrote a few stories and emailed them as gifts to friends. They in turn urged me to keep writing and send them more. In particular, I want to thank Terry Jones, Jack Rodman, Doug and Susan Jewett, Phillip Stein, Bruce and Betty Carter, Kay Knapton, Walter Liang, Fiona and Jim Jackson, Susan Bradley, Annie Brixner, Darcy Macdonald, Karen Stern, Kelly Scott, and Lisa Cavallari. They are all loyal yoga students, as well as friends. For years I have been regaling them during class with anecdotes, which some have heard more than once. For them to appreciate reading these amplified accounts has meant a lot.

I sent a number of these stories to my former college roommate and faithful friend, Bob Small. A fine writer, Bob politely reminded me of the sometimes subtle differences in correct usage of the verbs "take" and "bring," while reading my more linear (first) memoir, *Cutting Out: The Making and Unmaking of a Surgeon* in its entirety and penning a fine Afterword for the book, soon to be published.

Jerry Spinelli, one of my favorite authors ever, was kind enough to praise my pieces, sent to him one after another—despite the objections of my wife, who felt that I was taking up too much of his time. He told me that he read "Nice Try" to his wife, Eileen, a celebrated author of children's books, by the fire on a snowy winter's evening. I am grateful for Jerry's Foreword.

My musical friends, including Glenn Frank, Liz Talley, Gail Neil, Miriam Shames, Mike Crusoe, Steve Fissel, Teri Towe, Rick Peiser, Phil Ruggiero, Russell Walden, and Melinda Bargreen—all especially near and dear to my heart—have each read a number of my vignettes and essays. I am greatly indebted to Russ and Melinda in particular for the insightful and laudatory remarks that I am honored to include in this book.

Paul "Hutch" Raymer, novelist, blogger, home maintenance guru, and classmate from K-12 years, has been particularly kind in comparing my work to that of Native American wisemen. I would have thought "wise guys" might have been more apt, but I welcome his suggestion nonetheless!

Walter Brewster, arguably the most put-upon man in New York City, made it all the way through my book, and efficiently got to the nub of what it's about, as he does with the endless complaints that land on his desk.

Always there, in the back of my head, are the words and inspiration of my yoga guru, who will be embarrassed to have herself thus described. Catherine Munroe taught me the right way to teach yoga and accepted me for who I am when I deviated from the norm. I am happy that she has enjoyed the yoga anecdotes herein.

Kathy Cain, a relatively new yoga student, herself a formidable talent expert, has read the entire book during her convalescence from surgery—hopefully as a tonic—and offered kind words of praise and encouragement.

There are so many others who have taken the time to read some of this stuff, and then have taken even more time to acknowledge its worth: neighbors, former classmates, friends of friends…You know who you are. Forgive me for not listing each of you by name. Heartfelt thanks.

The family got a taste of the contents with an opportunity to correct me on a few details and to plead with me to go easier on them, which of course I preferred not to do.

I am particularly grateful to Father Dan Grigassy, a Franciscan friar, scholar, and treasured, non-judgmental cousin by marriage, who has written an erudite assessment of what this book has to offer in a few well-crafted words.

I thank Irving Berlin for his optimism in "Let's Have

Another Cup o'Coffee," which mirrors my own outlook on life. Better times are ahead. Believe me.

Oatley Kidder's clever, whimsical drawings grace the cover and numerous pages of this book. They are entirely consistent with what I have tried to convey in my writing.

Most of all, I am deeply indebted to Mary, far and away my better half, for her forbearance and invaluable help. Herself the author of nine books and an expert coach, she has proofread, edited, served as a sounding board, politely come up with more than a few better ways of expressing my meaning, and loved me throughout this journey, which I never would have undertaken without her.

All the while, Louis le Premier du Lac sat at my side, often placing his head on the side of the laptop as I typed, patiently waiting for a pat, a scratch, or a walk. My Muse.

As I completed the final iteration of this book for submission, a vivid rainbow suddenly appeared on a globe bookend across the room from me. A message of approval from my two angels, ZsaZsa and minette, that everything was right in my world of words. This work was done.

About the Author

James K. Weber, M.D., like most authors, writes about the things he knows. This book proves that he knows a lot about a lot of things. Back when he was a practicing surgeon, he wrote about weight loss surgery. More recently, he hearkened back to his considerable exposure to New York City society to co-write a book about manners with his wife, an expert on the subject. His book about changing careers and reuniting with the ever-polite love of his life, *Cutting Out: The Making and Unmaking of a Surgeon* is forthcoming.

Meanwhile, in this book, he gives the reader glimpses of his intriguing life, plenty to think about, and lots of laughs. Preferring to look at the bright side, he urges readers to stay alert to life's myriad possibilities. The next best thing just might be around the corner. You never know. You may be holding it in your hand right now.

www.prescriptionyoga.com

About the Illustrator

Oatley Kidder is a lifelong learner and fearless adventurer, both personally and artistically. When free from illustrating books, painting murals, or sculpting, she can be found teaching skateboarding or exploring the woods (where she might be harder to find). Her prodigious artistic gifts have been recognized with awards and in solo shows spanning both coasts.

9 781665 708548